CW00521398

From LUCKNOW *to* LUTYENS

THE POWER AND PLIGHT OF UTTAR PRADESH

From LUCKNOW *to* LUTYENS

ABHIGYAN PRAKASH

HarperCollins *Publishers* India

First published in India by HarperCollins *Publishers* 2022
Building No. 10, Tower A, 4th Floor, DLF Cyber City, Phase II
Gurugram, Haryana 122002
www.harpercollins.co.in

2 4 6 8 10 9 7 5 3 1

P-ISBN: 978-93-5489-575-3
E-ISBN: 978-93-5489-400-8

Cover design: Gavin Morris
Cover images: iStock and Shutterstock

Typeset in 12/16 Adobe Garamond at
Manipal Technologies Limited, Manipal

Printed and bound at
Thomson Press (India) Ltd

HarperCollinsIn

Dedicated to my mother, Rama Bajpai

Contents

Preface

Why I Wrote This Book

Why did I want to write this book? It was a question that constantly came to mind as I worked on it. The answer, of course, is deep and complex, and several aspects of it bothered me deeply for many years. That I was from Uttar Pradesh, born in Banaras (Kashi or Varanasi) and brought up in Lucknow, and that I had put behind me a good number of years at work and had grown personally, were good enough reasons for me to look at India's most politically powerful state, one that has supplied the biggest names and most prominent prime ministers in Indian politics. And that, despite UP's central importance in the Indian scheme of things, in post-Independence India it was still an underdeveloped state, far, far from realizing its full potential for impactful and inclusive socio-political and economic growth. This was puzzling and made me curious about exploring its modern history.

The deep awareness that I am from Uttar Pradesh actually began when I was living outside of it, in one of the most energetic and enigmatic of Indian cities, Mumbai. The journey of this book in fact begins from Mumbai. I had of course never imagined that one day I would land up in this intriguing and charismatic city. But in 2003, I found myself working in Mumbai, setting up part of NDTV India's operations there.

The initial reason that got me to Mumbai was very painful and very personal. I was working in Delhi at the time but had to keep visiting Mumbai to attend to a family matter. Over time, my visits to the city became more frequent, and I was meeting many more people there. Several of those friendships continue to date.

I met a range of people for various reasons, but the focus remained my family problems and responsibilities. Still, I was subconsciously absorbing the city and its energies. Its atmosphere, its chaos, its traffic and of course the fact that it literally does not sleep at night, which was for me something I had never encountered anywhere in India, all grew on me. Soon I was going to actually live and work in the city—which was in itself the experience of a lifetime.

But the most interesting and alluring thing I encountered in Mumbai during this tough time was the city's spoken Hindi, the Mumbai Hindi. Later, as I extensively travelled in the state of Maharashtra, I figured that the 'Mumbaiya' Hindi was not only fascinating but unique, as this Hindi was not spoken anywhere else in the state. It was fascinating in many ways because, as popularized by Bollywood, it could be both affectionate and rude as and when it needed to be. It is easily among the most unique flavours of Hindi that can be found anywhere outside the Hindi heartland where I come from, having taken its own routes and means of expression.

Having grown up in Lucknow under the influence of a Hindi and Sanskrit scholar-writer for a mother and many gurus and ustads during my training in the tabla, I was fairly equipped with spoken Hindustani, with the right amalgamation and balance of Hindi and Urdu—a 'zabaan' spoken in Lukhnauaa style. From there, the transition to Mumbaiya Hindi via Delhi's Punjabi Hindi influence was extremely fascinating for me. At the very outset it was clear to me that my adaptability in terms of language would not be exceptionally high. Rather, I would always struggle to get the fluency and pauses at the right junctures when I attempted to speak these other dialects. And it was exactly so. But I simply loved who I was and was very proud of my roots.

Seen through the prism of Mumbai city and society, I was a 'Bhaiya'. This is what hit me hard first during my early days of struggle in the city. Sometimes the word would be thrown at you in a blunt and derogatory manner. And this for me was the turning point of what I like to call '*thinking UP*'—thinking about UP, where I come from, as my reference point. Many individuals from my state had made noble and laudable contributions to Mumbai city and had achieved great heights in their fields; and the cosmopolitan city of Mumbai had accepted and embraced them in totality. Yet, for scores of people from my state who constituted part of the workforce in the city, eking out their livelihood by means of labour and other blue-collar jobs, deep discomfort and rejection were their lot. My understanding of this pain and conflict was becoming more acute with every visit to the city.

Soon came the turning point in my professional life. NDTV was planning to send some of its key faces to set up its Mumbai operations and the launch was set for April 2003. The office was now well aware that I was, for personal reasons, a regular visitor to the city. There was a big investigative story that my team was already working on, to be broadcast at the launch of the NDTV English and Hindi channels. It happened that an outstanding reporter, Sanjay Singh, in my team had broken the Telgi scam, involving corruption at the highest levels in the police; this fake stamp paper racket shook the entire police hierarchy of Maharashtra at that time. For me, the coverage of this scam entailed many interesting and fascinating stories, but that's for another time.

To come back to '*thinking UP*', something that had already begun to churn in my mind, one of the first few functions I was invited to speak at was a '*Me Mumbaikar* (I'm a Mumbaikar, in Marathi)' campaign of the Shiv Sena. It was organized by Sanjay Nirupam, a politician originally from Bihar but a Shiv Sainik who had also held an editorial position in the Sena's mouthpiece *Saamna.* (He later moved on from the Shiv Sena to the Congress.) I had barely been a few days in the city in my new avatar at work when a campaign against north Indians swept Mumbai. The north Indians in the city, who constituted an enormous workforce consisting of autorickshaw and taxi drivers and workers in many other capacities, were being accused of taking away opportunities from Maharashtrians. As I was new in the city, at the function I said on a lighter note, 'I have just moved from the north and I should immediately pack my bags and go back because in all probability I am taking away someone's job opportunity!' But I did get the sense that this anti-north Indian movement would become a larger issue and not just remain the subject of a seminar.

And it did reach violent proportions and was rightly and widely condemned all over the country, including in Parliament. It was Raj Thackeray who gave it a violent turn, with his men targeting taxi drivers who were from UP and Bihar. And this made for a very ugly tear in the cosmopolitan fabric of Mumbai. The issue was debated across the country. Politicians from UP and Bihar were angry and vocal about what was happening in Mumbai. It was against the basic Indian democratic ethos, which acknowledges that every Indian has the right to live and find work for himself and his family in any part of the country. There could not be any socio-political objections to that, surely.

Though the arguments of the Sena (and later the more violent Maharashtra Navnirman Sena, MNS, which was formed by Raj Thackeray in 2006) were completely unjustified, they did raise many questions in my mind, sending me back to '*thinking UP*'. The Maharahstrian politicians held that the city was bursting at the seams with people from outside the state and what it needed from outside were '*skilled people*'. So, the divide being created was clearly between 'skilled' and 'non-skilled'; they did not want non-skilled manpower from outside the state. But the reality was that the Sena and MNS had very strong labour unions in the city. So, the state's own people constituted the strongest workforce.

What was also conveniently overlooked, naturally for political reasons, was that there was also very significant intra-state immigration to Mumbai. Those coming from different parts of Maharashtra to look for work in the city, as also those from any other part of the country, were not to be questioned. In the meantime, several north Indian organizations also sprang up but did not make any significant impact. During this time, I spoke to my reporters, who understood the nuances of the migrant issue better than me, and asked them to work on a series of reports to debate the migrant issue properly and to bring out the basic character of the inclusivity of Mumbai. The result of these discussions was '*Mumbai Kiski*', a series on the success stories of 'outsiders' in the city, and my own show 'Mumbai Central', both of which did very well for the channel.

During all these happenings and activities, one root question continued to bother me about my own state: *why does India's most politically powerful state, Uttar Pradesh, remain so underdeveloped?* For people from all strata of society in UP, after India's economic liberalization which began in 1991, opportunities to earn a better livelihood lay outside their state. This way they could at least send back money to their homes in UP. And one such key centre of employment and opportunity was Mumbai.

While writing this book, as I dealt with the caste and communal politics of UP laced with horror stories of crime and politics, I could see how they threw light on the troublesome issues of Mumbai too. But, though the problems of UP may have had a bearing on matters in Mumbai, the reactions they engendered in the metropolis, of attacking and abusing north Indians, are not acceptable and cannot be justified in any manner.

At the onset of the Covid-19 pandemic in 2020, the abrupt announcement of the first lockdown brought in the most disturbing pictures of migrant labourers leaving their cities of work and walking back thousands of kilometres to reach their homes in UP and elsewhere, unsure as to whether they could survive in places like Mumbai with no job and no clue as to when work would resume. This led to discussions in the Yogi Adityanath government of UP about conducting a skill-mapping exercise in the state. To me it brought back memories of the anti-north-Indian wave in Mumbai. Around me I could see so many migrants in the city with multiple skills—the reason for the exercise that the UP government was planning had been there right in front of my eyes even in 2003.

The plight of humanity across India during the pandemic made me think: if those who ran the government in Uttar Pradesh had thought of skill mapping and creation of reasonable employment within the state thirty or forty years ago, surely the issue of migrants in Mumbai would have been very different. There would have been much better social respect and recognition for the 'Bhaiya'.

A few years later, work made me return to Delhi. But once you have been in Mumbai, it remains in you, growing in your heart. It is still there with me and will always be there with me. So, naturally, I stayed in contact with Mumbai always.

In the meantime, the migrant issue kept simmering and soon came a flashpoint, not providing a pretty picture of Mumbai to the rest of the country. On 3 February 2008, there were attacks on people from Uttar Pradesh and Bihar when clashes between Raj Thackeray's MNS and the Samajwadi Party (SP) of UP turned violent at Dadar in Mumbai. It was alleged that the clashes began when MNS workers tried to attack their counterparts in the Samajwadi Party who were proceeding to attend a rally. Raj Thackeray, nephew of the Shiv Sena founder Bal Thackeray, had become a central figure in this anti-north-Indian movement. Raj had left the Shiv Sena and formed his own party, the MNS, after Uddhav Thackeray—Bal Thackeray's son, who eventually became the chief minister of Maharashtra in 2019—was chosen to lead the Sena. Raj's style of public speaking was similar to Bal Thackeray's. In defending his party, Raj had then said that the attacks were a reaction to the provocative and unnecessary show of strength and uncontrolled political and cultural *dadagiri* (bullying) by immigrants from UP and Bihar and their leaders in Mumbai.

Raj was clearly trying to occupy all the space in politics on this issue and even went on target Amitabh Bachchan as a UP-ite who had achieved everything in Mumbai and Bollywood but only talked about UP. This, in fact, did not go down well even with his own uncle Bal Thackeray, who was a well-known friend of Amitabh Bachchan's. And Bachchan too used to often mention in public that Bal Thackeray was his friend and guide. MNS workers also targeted the Chhat Puja celebration by Biharis in the city; Raj's statements were now clearly hurting the sentiments of north Indians. In 2003, I had attended a Chhat Puja function organized by Sanjay Nirupam at Juhu beach. There was a massive turnout, and surely no politician worth his salt should criticize any such expression of faith.

Criticized for taking little action during these episodes, the state government, consisting of the Congress and Sharad Pawar's

Nationalist Congress Party (NCP), arrested both Raj Thackeray and Abu Azmi of the SP on 13 February 2008, on charges of instigating violence and causing communal disturbance. Although both were released, with a gag order against making inflammatory remarks that could cause communal disturbance, the tension in the city was palpable. And this tension sent its tremors through the Hindi heartland, particularly in Uttar Pradesh. The chief minister at the time in UP was Mayawati.

But the issue was far from over. The news that Raj Thackeray was going to be arrested angered his supporters. North Indians and their properties became the targets of their ire. Reports of attacks on north Indians by MNS workers started pouring in not only from Mumbai but also from Pune, Amravati, Beed and Nashik. The big point I wish to bring attention to is that this resulted in nearly 25,000 north Indian workers fleeing Pune and another 15,000 leaving Nashik. The final impact of this flight of migrants was on business, the exodus leading to acute worker shortage, which affected local industries badly. Analysts then pegged the financial losses of those few weeks at Rs 500–700 crore. This was an indication to me of the wealth generation the migrants were capable of and could have generated in their own state, given the right opportunities there.

As I detail in this book later, under the impact of its politics, there were many parameters of holistic socio-economic development on which UP had failed to impress. And many other states had grown much faster than UP on several fronts.

What further followed in Mumbai was very vulgar and created an uproar all across India. After a few months of lull, on 19 October 2008, MNS workers beat up north Indian candidates appearing for the All-India Railway Recruitment Board entrance exams in Mumbai. Then, an incident happened which shook everyone. On 28 October that year, a labourer from Uttar Pradesh was lynched in a Mumbai local commuter train. This was anti-migrant politics at its worst. In 1966 too, when Bal Thackeray had formed the Shiv Sena, it was centred on the sentiment of 'sons of the soil', or opportunities only for the '*Marathi manoos*'.

The city-centric anti-migrant issue was a national one now. At the Centre, the Congress-led United Progressive Alliance (UPA) government was under huge pressure, especially from its allies, to dismiss the Congress–NCP government in the state. There was a phase when appeals for cancellation of trains to Maharashtra reached the Centre and Lalu Prasad Yadav, then railway minister, threatened to cancel trains to those regions in the state where railway passengers and property had been targeted.

There was bound to be pressure on the Chief Minister of Maharashtra Vilasrao Deshmukh, and of course on the Maratha strongman of the NCP, Sharad Pawar himself. Naturally, leaders like Mayawati were very vocal. Maharashtra Deputy Chief Minister R.R. Patil came in for massive flak during a discussion in Parliament for his use of the phrase 'bullet for bullet' in response to the killing of a Bihari youth in a Mumbai bus. In the furious exchange of words, a very important point was made: well over 40 per cent of the workforce in Mumbai consisted of those who were not born Maharashtrian. It was pointed out that they had contributed in a big way to the economy of the city through their hard work and labour. What might not the same UP workforce, today toiling away not only in Mumbai but in different parts of the country, have accomplished in their home state, given the right opportunities?

As in many other public situations, there were different aspects of politics at play in this one too. The charge was even made that Raj Thackeray had the political backing of the state government of the time. Naturally, this was strongly refuted by the state's political establishment.

It took some time for the city to recover. But being the city that it is, Mumbai recovers—a quality it has displayed in many other situations too. Whenever I travelled in Mumbai, I would chat with cab and auto drivers from UP and ask them how things had changed. Being a 'Bhaiya' was, after all, something of a derogatory thing, opening one to political and social condemnation. But they were all clear. They would still ask their relatives back home in their villages to come to Mumbai. And they would often say, 'Whatever the situation or struggle may be, *yeh shahar Mumbai kisi ko raat ko bhukha nahin sone deta*'—this city will ensure that no one goes to sleep hungry. It's the oldest and the most famous line you will hear from someone from outside Mumbai about the city. So, as I write this book, '*thinking UP*' in my mind, it does occur to me to ask myself: can the same be said about my state and its state of affairs? There has been improvement, yes, undoubtedly, but not to the extent one wishes.

I was born in the early 1970s in Banaras in Kalika Gali, a very famous lane close to the Kashi Vishwanath mandir of Lord Shiva, a temple visited by lakhs and lakhs of devotees every year. The journey of my life begins from here, and also the journey of my learning Indian classical music. I began to learn the tabla, one of those most glorious of percussion instruments, at a very early age. I would walk across the famous gali that leads to the Kashi Vishwanath temple, and further ahead from there to the Dashashwamedh Ghat on the Ganga. I would then cross the ghat. My memories of that walk are still very clear.

I would enter the well-known place next to the ghat used by Bengalis, known as the Bengali tola mohalla. And here, amidst the many multistoreyed, old, yet beautiful structures around, was the house of my tabla guru, Dr Ashutosh Bhattacharya, also respectfully known as Ashu Babu. He was a tabla great of the Banaras gharana with exemplary command of the 'Banaras Baaj'. Like many of his contemporaries of that time, he was also a renowned homeopathic doctor. And in the cultural circles of Kashi, he was also well known as 'Guru Bhai' of the sitar maestro Pandit Ravi Shankar. So, indeed, I was privileged as a young boy.

On top of the house was the learning and practice (riyaz) area, accessed by a steep flight of stairs. There were no lifts of course. (It is good to know that many of the buildings are now being altered to have lifts.) The learning hall had large, old wood-carved windows and they opened to a delightful view of the Ganga right in front of us, with sailing boats on the waters.

The clearest memory I have of learning at Ashu Babu's as a kid is that we children were given a wooden table to practise on, and not the full-fledged drums with their amazing tonality. The practice on the wooden table was for our middle fingers to take proper shape before we handled the instrument itself and to understand the importance of beats (*taal*), the use of precise mathematical calculations and, of course, to learn to appreciate sound and tone (*sur*) to lay the foundation for advanced lessons. So, this was my life's beginning in Banaras, at least as far as my memory can go; and along with this I was attending a convent school. So, it was a good balance of modern and traditional Indian influences that I had.

Banaras has a deep and vast history of culture and civilization. Kashi is Baba Bholenath Lord Shiva's city. It's also a city of intellects, music learning and the great Saint Kabir. And for me and everyone else who hails from there, Banaras is also about delightful and delicious food—churned out by the local food outlets in the lanes and by-lanes. And it is the home of the legendary Banarasi *paan*, which of course I was never allowed to eat as a child. But when I grew up and had my first *paan*, the taste of it would remain with me for the rest of my life. Later, over the years, I came to realize how big the *paan*-eating culture in UP was and how it was passed down the generations, the younger ones of which were eating *paan masala*—a top favourite among the *chamchas* (flunkies) of UP politicians—making for a not-so-very-pleasant sight when they speak with their mouths full or when they spit. As the original *paan* was being replaced with *gutka* (*paan masala*), it appeared to be coinciding with the multiple transitions in UP politics itself—the subject of this book.

My father's work took the family to Lucknow, and our Banaras days ended. Lucknow was another city full of learning, culture, music, food and a great nawabi heritage of its own. The over-politicization of Lucknow city, in my view, happened in the late 1980s, overwhelming its cultural past in the 1990s in particular. Yet, parts of the city of nawabs retained their charm while the city itself passed through massive political movements and upheavals. The tonality, language and *tahzeeb* (etiquette in speech) it once had seem to have undergone a change too.

I was young enough to go with the cultural transition that moving from Banaras to Lucknow meant. But there was continuity too. Born to a Sanskrit scholar-writer-poet mother, my education at home in a literary environment continued. My tabla lessons also continued. I was soon in the hands of the last doyen of the Lucknow gharana, Ustad Ashfaq Hussain Khan Saheb. His softness and rhythm of playing the instrument, so classical of the Lucknow gharana, left a deep impression on me. He was also a gentleman who showered immense love and affection on me and made me feel very special as a child. While my training with him continued, I found it difficult to manage school, where I had already become known as a tabla player, and my tabla classes at my Ustad's house, which was a considerable distance from school.

So, a midway solution had to be found, and that's how I entered the legendary Bhatkhande Music Institute in Lucknow. It was originally the Marris College of Hindustani Music during the British period but was later named after the great Maharashtrian musician and academician Vishnu Digambar Bhatkhande. The guru I found here was Pandit Sheetal Prasad Mishra, a tutor as lovable and affectionate as my Ustad earlier. This solved my problem of attending music classes after school. Earlier I had to rush to the Ustad's house straight from school because he followed a puritanical pattern of timing and learning in the *guru-shishya parampara* tradition, which had to be honoured. But, while my Bhatkhande classes continued, so did the blessings and teachings of my Ustad, as I continued to learn from him if he was available on the weekends. These were the years when music, along with my studies, and of course cricket, meant everything in my life.

To my surprise, opportunities to write for newspapers came my way. I was excited, but the only thing I would be able to competently review or analyse would be Indian classical music. And that is what I began with. So those were my baby steps in journalism—music reviews for the *Times of India* and some reporting for the *Pioneer*. Those were also very politically tumultuous times in UP and Lucknow. The roads of the city, including the main thoroughfare connecting the famous Charbagh railway station to the rest of the city, witnessed a lot of activity from the late 1980s onwards. These I have elaborated on later in the book.

One memorable incident was my first real-life sighting of a politician, and that was Vishwanath Pratap Singh. My friends and I were actually very irritated that day; we were out on bicycles and were not able to negotiate the overcrowded Hazratganj crossing because there was V.P. Singh with hordes of supporters blocking all traffic. Even rickshaws and people on cycles like me were being stopped. His supporters were loudly raising slogans: '*Raja nahi fakir hai, desh ki takdeer hai.*' Little did I know or care that these were public protests against then Prime Minister Rajiv Gandhi in whose cabinet V.P. Singh had been a key person. After getting out of the government, V.P. Singh was accusing Gandhi of corruption. At that time, I had no visions of being a political reporter, less so one covering many such events even outside UP. All I remember was the irritation on my friends' faces and mine. Many, many years later I realized that V.P. Singh may have spoilt our cricket match that day but surely won his political match against Rajiv Gandhi. What I saw that day was my first dose of UP politics in the heart of Lucknow at its dramatic best. V.P. Singh had also been chief minister of Uttar Pradesh, so he had considerable following in the state, which was evident to me that day. But at the time I had zero interest, knowledge and understanding of politics. On the drama quotient, though, V.P. Singh's blocking of traffic that day in the middle of Hazratganj did not even qualify as a trailer for the movies that were to appear in the future. I have described many such 'movies' in this book.

Any issue that pertains to Uttar Pradesh is complicated and full of its own contradictions, and there is opportunistic politics to be detected every step of the way. So, the reason I have titled the first chapter 'The Fake Agenda' is that all governments, on the face of it, declare that development of the state is their chief concern. But, right from the beginning, those full-page newspaper advertisements describing government programmes and announcements, containing photographs of prominent leaders, have been only made for political gains. They are part of the agenda of making the right political moves but never actually delivering real development to the people. These newspaper advertisements were later supplemented by TV ads, where the key catch-word was 'vikas'—development—but as is widely known and understood, that never became a reality. If it had, the people of the state would not have voted out government after government. Another unique aspect of UP politics, in the context of the fake agenda, is that for decades since Independence, no chief minister had ever been able to complete a full term for his vision for positive transformation of the state to be implemented. Such was the politics of the state. In fact, it was Mayawati, who came to power in May 2007, who was the first chief minister in the state to last a full term. She was followed by Akhilesh Yadav in 2012, who was followed by Yogi Adityanath in 2017.

The deepest and darkest reality of Indian politics is caste. And, just like in the rest of the country, it is also the reality of UP. Caste has to be accepted to understand its impact. From the time of the British, different caste equations were understood, analysed and worked upon for reasons of governance, and this continued in post-Independence India and, of course, in UP. Every political party worked to make sure that its caste base remained with it. Until the present day, and for a long time now, election tickets have been distributed among candidates—with exceptions, of course—based on caste equations in the constituency in question and the candidate's caste representation, which is crucial for his or her own winnability. Election after election, when analysed, has proven that when the caste arithmetic clicks well for a political party, it can and has given winning electoral results. The formula is now considered time-tested. The chapter on caste details how the political fortunes of all the major players in UP politics—from the time of Congress dominance to the rise of the Bharatiya Janata Party (BJP), including the Mandal-Kamandal era and the subsequent rise of Mulayam Singh Yadav and Mayawati—hinge on those caste combinations that have been crucial for their times.

In the process of researching and analysing varying aspects of Uttar Pradesh pertinent to the book, the most unique of them,

I discovered, turns out to be the criminalization of politics. The entry of criminals in Indian politics, as seen both inside and outside of Parliament, is a very old phenomenon, but in UP its history and incidences have unique ramifications, and one of them is the caste angle to the rise of criminality in politics in the state. This is evident just from eastern UP's sagas of crime and politics. It was the Brahmin-versus-Thakur conflict in this region that impacted both the politics and crimes of its times. Among the political mafia, names like Harishankar Tiwari who, ironically, wore a Gandhi cap, were later to impact many government formations and their political moves in UP. Tiwari even became a science and technology minister in the UP cabinet.

Then there are the stories of caste oppression, resulting in those oppressed by the upper castes turning to the gun to exact revenge, in the process becoming dacoits representing their caste. The best known of these stories is that of Phoolan Devi, a woman from the backward caste of Nishad. She was raped by men from the Thakur caste, and she exacted revenge on them, wielding a gun herself and becoming a dacoit. She became a member of Parliament too. There are other similar stories, such as those of Dadua and Nirbhay Singh Gujjar, which are all telling of caste oppression. Ill-treated by the upper castes, these people picked up the rifle for revenge and survival, also becoming a figure of hope for their respective castes in Robin Hood style. What is most important to mention here is that they all developed considerable political clout, forcing politicians of different political hues to seek their support from time to time.

Later, the spotlight in the criminal world moved to a young Brahmin face, that of Shri Prakash Shukla. His rise was meteoric in the UP crime world, allegedly backed by the old Brahmin mafia names like Harishankar Tiwari. But soon it became apparent that the same Shri Prakash Shukla had become a nemesis for the casteist politicians who had at one point backed him to get him to the standing he had attained. Shri Prakash Shukla became hugely infamous for his contract killings in broad daylight. He was even alleged to have taken a contract to kill then UP chief minister Kalyan Singh. These were perhaps the darkest times of caste-based criminalization in UP politics. Eventually, the police were pressed into action and Shri Prakash Shukla was killed in an 'encounter' in Ghaziabad in 1998. This is not the last of such stories. Let us not forget the more recent case of Vikas Dubey, whose handling by the UP police came under severe criticism. Vikas Dubey's is a stand-out example of caste-based criminalization in politics because his alleged encounter killing by the UP police resulted in a Brahmin backlash against Chief Minister Yogi Adityanath, who is a Thakur. In short, the caste–criminality nexus still very much exists in UP.

To study UP in a national context is impossible without also studying the Congress, its days of dominance and its days of collapse in the state, after which it has never returned to date. The reason for the Congress collapse seems very clearly in alignment with the national political mood. With the rise of Mandal and, parallelly, Kamandal politics, the space for the Congress sharply shrank in UP from the 1990s onwards. Post-Mandal politics created key players from backward castes like Mulayam Singh Yadav and Mayawati; and of course, with the Ram Janmabhoomi movement since the early 1990s, the BJP walked strong with its pro-Hindutva upper-caste appeal. Through most of the 1980s, most of the Congress chief ministers were either prominent Brahmin or Thakur faces. This being so, it's simple to understand how the Congress lost this base to the BJP while Mulayam Singh Yadav, with the support of Muslims, founded a new Muslim–backward combination and Kanshi Ram strategized for the Dalits to back the Bahujan Samaj Party (BSP) and its leader Mayawati. The Congress took the decision to open the locks at the Ram Janmabhoomi site in Ayodhya but did not manage to draw political mileage out of it. What characterized the 1990s was the polarization in politics along caste and communal lines, with each side working out its algorithms and rhetoric to create its own polarization planks. Again, an analysis of UP elections down the years proves that the polarization formula has worked time and again. Each party, while claiming inclusiveness, has left no stone unturned to use polarization to political benefit. Even statements made by the biggest of leaders down the years have been targeted to achieve this.

If there is one issue post-Mandal that changed the landscape of UP and India, it was undoubtedly Ayodhya. From the time the BJP adopted this issue in the form of a resolution at a meeting in Palampur, Himachal Pradesh, in 1989, it changed the electoral fortunes of the party forever. It is important to recall that since its inception in the 1980s in Mumbai, the BJP had struggled to find an issue it could put on the nation's centre stage so it could be seen as a national alternative to the Congress. Earlier, coalitions like the Janata Party were experimented with, but with its collapse the coalition option was never seen as a strong, clear alternative to the Congress. The V.P. Singh and Chandrashekhar coalitions too were perceived in the same way. They did form alternative governments, but not as a total alternative to the Congress. I discuss in detail how because of Ayodhya and its power politics, every year after 1989 witnessed the rise of the BJP. The party was so 'Ram bharose' that in 1991, even before the Babri Masjid demolition of 1992, it had formed a government under one of the most belligerent and iconic faces of the Ram Janmabhoomi movement, Kalyan Singh. One can clearly see what a turnaround this issue constituted for the BJP. From time to time, the party also ignored this issue under political compulsions, particularly during the period when Atal Bihari Vajpayee was the leader of the National Democratic Alliance (NDA), the first non-Congress government to manage a full term at the Centre. So, the BJP, according to its political needs, did the back and forth on Ayodhya, but it never dropped the issue fully. And finally, with the Supreme Court judgement of 9 November 2019, Prime Minister Narendra Modi of the BJP, on 5 August 2020, went ahead with the *bhoomipujan* of the promised Lord Ram temple in Ayodhya.

While writing this book, a key feature of UP politics that kept coming to mind was the *ilakaas*—the bastions—of some of the biggest names in Indian politics. When we travel across UP, which I did many times over two decades, we actually pass through these 'bastions' one after the other, each associated with high-profile names who have lorded over Indian politics from time to time. And yet we find UP on the whole underdeveloped. What was the reason for this, and why did that happen? One straight conclusion is that as and when the bastions were lost by one politician to another, any work that was being done by the predecessor was either stopped or took a U-turn. And this to me is the irony of UP, where development takes a back seat because a big name loses his 'bastion'. There are many examples of this in this book. I have noticed that many political bastions in India that have been retained by political families and their representatives have naturally received special attention, resulting in the same families winning the same Lok Sabha seat election after election. But I have also noticed that once lost by them, progress in that region soon comes to a halt.

Countless are the *dalbadlu* jokes which are to be found in every state, and in UP in every lane practically. These jokes lend so much fun and colour to UP politics. I could find no English word to precisely describe the sense and nuance of the word *dalbadlu*, so I thought I'd coin my own term—'switcher'. Switchers cannot and should not ever be taken lightly in UP politics. If you look at the decade of the 1990s in particular, their role in making and unmaking governments was unbelievably crucial, and because they were willing to switch sides, they had great bargaining power and could land up on any side of the political divide. And every party accepted them without guilt, and without any question of morality bothering them, as the switchers helped form governments. This also resulted in the unbelievable size of ministerial cabinets in UP. The biggest example of it was the record-breaking ninety-four-minister cabinet of the Kalyan Singh government in 1997, with Harishankar Tiwari, a known member of the political mafia from Gorakhpur, becoming science and technology minister. Tiwari, like many a switcher, was a classic face that proved it could be on any side, from the Congress to the BJP. The switchers of the 1990s were unique 'properties' to be traded politically and were the subject of much discussion and debate in UP politics at the time.

If we just look at eastern UP, the very significant and politically powerful region of the state, one can see that it has the poorest parts of the state that have been the most crime-ridden. This region has the lowest per capita agri-income, and that has been the story for many years despite India's economic reforms. In fact, that has also been the story of another region in UP, Bundelkhand. The reason I specially mention eastern UP and Bundelkhand is that they represent the deep-seated agrarian crisis that the state is in; agricultural reforms for farmers have not been working fully at the grassroots level. The government schemes for them, as in the rest of India, have been many, and so have been the government grants for them from taxpayers' money. Despite all this, farmers in these regions have been battling agrarian crises for generations now. Strangely, neither the central nor state schemes benefit those who need them the most.

In my years of travelling across India reporting on rural issues and farmer distress, one story always stands out. In May 2016, I wrote a column titled 'Who will dry Radha's tears?' for a leading publication. Radha was a woman in a village in Mathura whose husband died of a heart attack after learning that their crop was destroyed by unseasonal rains. Why was he hit badly by this trauma? The answer is that he, like thousands of others in India, was a landless farmer. He worked someone else's land, borrowing money from a local lender to do so, and if things went wrong, there was no way he could pay back the loan. And, as he did not own the land, the government schemes had never reached him for years. This is the plight and distress of the landless farmer, not only in UP but in many other parts of India too. It is a tragedy that has still not been completely addressed by the governments of the day.

These are some of the issues I hope to do justice to in this book as I take a macro view of the affairs of the state in the context of national politics—'from Lucknow to Lutyens', in a sense.

1
The Political Change Agenda

The politics of Uttar Pradesh, India's most populous and perhaps most important of states electorally, has been plagued by caste, class and communal factors throughout the post-Independence era. When the Congress party, which was ruling the roost for years and had absolute dominance in the country, began tasting decline in the 1980s, it made clear way for a new kind of politics—one of polarization—in the state.

Dalits and Muslims were finding a new political identity in the state through the BSP of Kanshi Ram and Mayawati and the SP of Mulayam Singh Yadav. The latter, besides being seen as a Yadav leader, was also quickly criticized by some opposition parties for his Muslim-centric approach to politics.[1] Not to be left behind in the race for political supremacy, the BJP, essentially an upper-caste Brahmin–Baniya party,[2] decided to thrust in its brand of Hindutva at the opportune moment. The Ram Mandir movement, eventually leading to the Babri Masjid demolition in 1992 by Hindutva elements, gave further momentum to its Hindutva agenda. The overall result of this development was that the state increasingly became a fertile ground for identity politics revolving around the Hindutva, Mandal and Dalit factors.

The entity that suffered the most in this aggressive rush for power was UP itself, which was left mercilessly divided on caste and communal lines. Unfortunately, this very dividing line continues to hold the key to its politics even decades later. It has been a hysterical rollercoaster ride between the politics of Mandal and Kamandal ever since. The history of UP politics provides a clear background to the influences that the numerous regime changes and the myriad leaders with their unique brand of politics have had in this state.

The Indian National Congress was at the helm in Indian politics, uninterrupted, from the period 1947 to 1966, marking an era of single-party dominance. Its winning streak was unbroken in the first three elections in the country, which were held in 1952, 1957 and 1962, and it secured massive majorities in the Lok Sabha as well as in most of the state legislative assemblies, emerging as a truly national party. The electorate seemed to have reposed its faith in the Congress leadership, seeing it as a party that could rise above party, sectarian and personal interests and was capable of laying the foundation of economic prosperity for the nascent republic. The charisma and popularity of Jawaharlal Nehru also contributed to the remarkable electoral performances of the party during this period. This monopoly at the Centre and the states was only briefly shaken in the period between 1957 and 1959, when a Communist Party of India (CPI)-led regime was elected to power in Kerala, only to be toppled by the Union government.

The Congress's cool complacency was rudely shaken in the general election of 1967, which is considered a watershed year in Indian politics. This fourth general election aptly came to be seen as the revolt of the masses. It radically changed the political map of India, to say the least. Its results reflected the disillusionment of the people with the Congress and at the same time marked the rise of new forces in Indian politics. The Congress monolith, which for so long had dominated the Indian political landscape, was badly mauled and left humbled.

The party was rejected by the electorate in nearly half of the sixteen states of the Union. Even at the Centre, it returned with a rather reduced majority. It won 280 seats, only twenty more than the halfway mark in the 520-member Lok Sabha. The only states that saw the Congress get an absolute majority were Andhra Pradesh, Assam, Gujarat, Haryana, Madhya Pradesh, Mysore, Tripura and Himachal Pradesh. The Congress also emerged as the single largest party in Bihar, Punjab, Rajasthan, UP and West Bengal. But in Kerala, Madras, Orissa and Delhi, it lost its primary position to the Communist Party of India (Marxist), the Dravida Munnetra Kazhagam (DMK), the Swatantra Party and the Bhartiya Jana Sangh (BJS) respectively. The debacle of the supposedly unshakeable and undefeatable Congress made headlines globally. The *Guardian*, in a news item titled 'Congress Dominance Dismantled', dated 18 February 1967, wrote:

> The elections now in progress in India are moving the country into a new stage in its constitutional evolution. For the first time, the result is not a foregone conclusion. In the central polling, certainly, the Congress will win majority big

> enough to ensure it another five years as the party governing India. But who can be sure about the state legislatures? The Congress is almost certain to lose in Kerala. Most observers seem to think it will lose in three or more states too.

The 1967 general election may, in a sense, be regarded as the harbinger of a new era in Indian politics, for it introduced what came to be known as 'Samyukta Vidhayak Dals'—or 'United Fronts'—in certain states, thus giving birth to coalition governments in UP, Bihar, Orissa, Kerala and some other states. However, thanks to the incompatibility of the constituent partners, as is often the case in any coalition of parties, they did not last long.

The tremendous impact of the sudden transformation in national politics sent ripples through the political waters in Uttar Pradesh. While in the first election to the UP Vidhan Sabha the Congress had secured an overwhelming majority with practically no opposition, the second election reduced the number of Congress MLAs by about 100 (from 388 to 286), not an insubstantial number. However, the Congress still had a comfortable majority and managed to pass the full five-year term. Incidentally, the most notable defeat in this election was that of Chandra Bhanu Gupta from Lucknow at the hands of Triloki Singh, a Praja Socialist Party (PSP) candidate, Gupta's erstwhile opponent in Congress politics.

This period witnessed a major rift within the Congress party in UP, which was now riven into two camps. One was headed by Dr Sampurnanand and the other by Chandra Bhanu Gupta. Their struggle for power in the party went on for so long that it eventually resulted in a gulf that could never be bridged. As a result of this ever-growing chasm within the party, the position of the Congress weakened to a large extent after the third election, held in 1962. Nevertheless, it still wasn't so weak that its influence could be dismissed just yet, as it continued to have a comfortable majority in the Vidhan Sabha. It was at this time that the Jana Sangh emerged as the second largest party in the state, with nearly 50 members.

It was the fourth Vidhan Sabha election of 1967 that truly dismantled the monopoly of the Congress in UP. For the first time in the history of the Vidhan Sabha, the Congress party failed to get an absolute majority. From bagging 90 per cent of the seats in the first election, the Congress party's tally now fell to a measly 47 per cent of seats. It won only 199 seats out of the total 425 in this game-changing election. Its prospects seemed even more diminished in light of the performance of the BJS, the precursor to the BJP, which won 98 seats. Also moving into the space left by the Congress was the Samyukta Socialist Party (SSP), which managed to get 44 seats in this election.

It was also after the fourth Vidhan Sabha election that the Jat leader Chaudhary Charan Singh broke his ties with the Congress and finally formed his own party, the Bhartiya Kranti Dal (BKD). Socialists like Ram Manohar Lohia and Raj Narain, and Nanaji Deshmukh from the Jana Sangh, supported him. In April 1967, Chaudhary Charan Singh was sworn in as chief minister of UP, as the head of the Samyukta Vidhayak Dal (SVD), a coalition which had allies ranging from the CPI(M) on the left to the BJS on the right, with the Republican Party of India, Swatantra Party, PSP and 22 independents in between. This was the BJS's first taste of power, an experience about which Nanaji Deshmukh subsequently wrote, 'Our party lost the image of a party with a difference. Our people rose as important leaders but … the party of workers was converted into a party of leaders.'[3]

The four years that followed Charan Singh's rise to power were rather tumultuous for the state. Those four years saw four chief ministers and two phases of President's rule. Despite emerging as the leader of the north Indian farmer communities such as the Jats, Yadavs, Gujars, Kurmis and other backward classes, and also of the Muslims, Charan Singh faced many problems in his government, mainly owing to a clash of interests between the coalition partners. SVD partner SSP began an 'Angrezi Hatao' (Ban English) movement, which resulted in two cabinet ministers courting arrest and resigning. Some other parties too withdrew from the coalition and, in February 1968, Charan Singh resigned, recommending dissolution of the assembly.

After a year of central rule, elections were held in 1969. The BKD won 98 seats and the Jana Sangh forty-nine. The Congress won 211 seats in the 425-member house, and Chandra Bhanu Gupta returned as CM. But his reign too didn't last long, as within a year of his coming to power the Congress split and Gupta lost his majority and resigned. February 1970 saw the return of Chaudhary Charan Singh, this time with the help of Indira Gandhi's Congress (R).

Unfortunately, this new phase too was riddled with problems. Charan Singh asked for the resignations of fourteen ministers belonging to the Congress (R) who, led by Kamalapati Tripathi, refused to resign. Charan Singh recommended the ministers' dismissal to the governor, B. Gopala Reddy, who instead asked

Charan Singh to resign. This move put UP under President's rule once again, even though only for a short spell. Elections were held once more, and Tribhuvan Narain Singh was sworn in as chief minister at the head of the SVD in October 1970. His was a government put together by leaders of the Congress (O), the old Congress guard that was opposed to Indira.

Tribhuvan Narain Singh's tenure was not meant to be, and he lasted barely five months in the chair. He suffered the ignominy of becoming one of the first chief ministers to lose an assembly by-election in the state (from Maniram in Gorakhpur in March 1971) and had to resign. Kamalapati Tripathi succeeded him and remained chief minister until June 1973, when a revolt by the Provincial Armed Constabulary in demand of better pay and work conditions forced him out of office. After a few months of President's rule yet again, Hemwati Nandan Bahuguna, a Garhwali Brahmin, became chief minister in November 1973. He resigned in November 1975 following differences with Sanjay Gandhi and was replaced by N.D. Tiwari, a Kumauni Brahmin, who was very close to Sanjay Gandhi at the time.

The Era of Caste and Identity Politics

The years from 1967 to 1973 were a period of intense churning in the politics of UP, when caste and other identity issues took precedence. This led to several significant changes in the style of UP politics. The most important among them was the emergence of new tensions with the entry into the political scene of a new socio-economic group consisting of backward castes, lower sections of the peasantry, landless labourers and state government employees. They brought to the fore new issues—land reforms, redistribution of wealth and increase in the pay scales for government employees. This movement of sorts led to the emergence of numerous caste associations, such as the Kshatriya Mahasabha and Kurmi Mahasabha, in state politics.

They tried to influence government decision-making in their own favour and adopted strategies towards this end, in accordance with the demands of the situation and the resources available. The emergence of identity politics in the state made caste and community assertions talking points. This new dimension of politics had many ramifications. One way to relate to this change in the politics of Uttar Pradesh was to track the electoral success of the Jana Sangh. As has been mentioned earlier, the ascendance of the Jana Sangh in UP was closely associated with the dismantling of the Congress monopoly in UP.

The Jana Sangh Story

It would be interesting and relevant to trace the genesis, growth and metamorphosis of the Jana Sangh down the years at this point. The Jana Sangh was largely an outcome of the Rashtriya Swayamsevak Sangh's (RSS) efforts to transform itself from a mass organization into an organization with a liberal and democratic outlook in the aftermath of India's Independence.[4]

When the ideological congruence between the Hindu Mahasabha and the RSS had begun to take place in the face of the contentious Partition question, the RSS had started to transform itself into a mass militant organization. To this end it needed a large number of strong youths as members. At that stage, it had to go beyond its *dvija* (members of the three social classes—Brahmins, Kshatriyas and Vaishyas) social base and recruit Shudra / Other Backward Classes (OBC) and Dalit youths.

After the Jana Sangh was formed, a section of Baniyas moved away from the Congress and joined it. The Jana Sangh now began to emerge as a Brahmin–Baniya party. Its social base was basically urban, supported as it was by these two castes which had urbanized themselves in the post-Independence period. The party mobilized enough money from temples and from the Baniya community and worked as a pressure group for traditional Brahmins and Baniyas. During that period, the Congress expanded its social base among the agrarian Shudra social forces. The Jana Sangh could never boast of such a social base.

With the dismantling of the monopoly of the Congress in UP, the Jana Sangh started articulating its electoral strategy around identity issues. Electoral support for the Jana Sangh in UP largely came from the merchants, shopkeepers and businessmen in the towns, and from the big landlords in the villages. In the early 1950s, in its first electoral contest in 1952, the Jana Sangh depended on a landlord party, the Praja Party, in UP. Landlords apart, the elements of the old Hindu Mahasabhas too provided the Jana Sangh a natural base. They succeeded in bringing into their fold a sizeable section of petty traders and businessmen, usually known by the umbrella term of Baniya. While the main voter base of the Jana Sangh consisted of these communities—

landlords, upper castes, petty traders and businessmen—the party also succeeded in spreading its base wider, registering a presence in both urban and rural areas. Moreover, the weakness of the ruling Congress propelled the Jana Sangh to its best performance until then in 1967, winning 98 seats.

Not wishing to confine itself to the Lok Sabha and state assembly elections, the party also tried to expand its base in the rural areas by contesting civic elections, giving out clear signals that it wanted to be perceived as a party of mass appeal. However, this desire came to naught; the Jana Sangh could not sustain the tempo because it was not the only party foraging for votes; numerous other parties too wanted to seize the opportunity left wide open by a marginalized Congress in order to get a foothold in UP.

In short, while back in the 1950s the support base and leadership of the Jana Sangh came from the elite upper castes, mainly in Oudh and central UP, it had by the 1970s shifted to the Hindu trading community in towns and the big landlords in the rural areas. The Jana Sangh support base mainly lay in the hill districts, the plateau region, and in the eastern and central plains of the state. In regional terms, these areas encompassed the districts of Bahraich, Basti and Gonda in the northern belt, and Sitapur, Lakhimpur Kheri and Hardoi in the central plains of UP. In 1967, the Jana Sangh expanded its base into the western plains but could not retain its gains there because of the rise of the BKD.

The fourth state assembly election of 1967 saw the Jana Sangh take up the cudgels for Hindutva. It supported the Gau Raksha Samiti to push for a complete ban on cow slaughter by the central government. In support of the demand, Jagat Guru Shankaracharya of Puri undertook a fast, which he eventually gave up on 31 January 1967 after a period of seventy-three days. Clearly, the Jana Sangh was supporting the cause to whip up sentiments among the Hindu masses so they would turn against the ruling party, the Congress. The Jana Sangh even tried to organize a campaign for implementation of Article 48 of the Constitution of India, which recommends the prohibition of slaughter of cows, calves, milch and draught cattle.

The Jana Sangh seemed to have found a strong agenda by now. In fact, as a partner in the SVD government of Uttar Pradesh, the Jana Sangh successfully pressured the coalition to pander to its various demands to meet its Hindu ideological outlook. For example, on 30 July 1967, the Jana Sangh insisted that the government should not accept the demand to make Urdu the second official language of the state. Applying enough pressure tactics, it threatened to quit the government. Urdu, according to Jana Sanghis, was not a language of India but was brought to the country by foreigners who tried to impose it on Indians. They were also of the firm opinion that the contemporary Muslim intellectual activities had their origins primarily in Aligarh Muslim University. So, they demanded that the Muslim character of the Aligarh Muslim University be erased by having it 'Indianized' and run like other universities in the country. Apparently, the Jana Sangh was in favour of Hindi and other regional languages as official languages for the respective states as opposed to English. The Sanghis wanted this implemented within a period of fifteen years.

But the party's Hindutva agenda turned out to be the reason for its downfall. The Jana Sangh's continual harping on Hindu identity issues led to the collapse of the non-Congress SVD government in 1968. The deputy CM and minister of education Ram Prakash Gupta, a former pracharak and a former deputy mayor of Lucknow, was accused of promoting Saraswati Shishu Mandir schools, while Ganga Bhakt Singh, the minister of cooperation and the public works department, was denounced for recruiting Hindu nationalist sympathizers to administrative posts.[5]

Several other factors worked against the party. For one, the Jana Sangh even articulated its economic policies around identity issues. As the party wanted the support of the urban Hindu middle class, it emphasized food, clothing and shelter as the most important economic issues in the country. Also, as the Hindu landlord in UP formed the main support base of the Jana Sangh, the party never gave its wholehearted support to land reforms. It was not against the abolition of the *jagirdari* and *zamindari* systems but wanted adequate compensation to be given to the landlords and enough land left for them. Apart from advocating a ban on cow slaughter, the party also wanted upgradation of the quality of cattle in the state in order to make cattle economic units of agriculture.

At this time, the Jana Sangh was the only political party in UP state politics that was asserting identity issues for electoral gains. But other players were soon to arrive on the scene, vehemently claiming to represent the interests of the lower or backward castes. The most decisive development in this respect was the emergence of Chaudhary Charan Singh in the politics of the Hindi heartland. He was highly influenced by Chhotu Ram, the chief architect of *kisan* (farmer) politics in Punjab, who advocated the idea of a *biradari* (brotherhood of peasants) among the Ahirs, Jats, Gujars and Rajputs, jointly referred to by the acronym AJGAR.

Charan Singh's Caste and Kisan Politics

The mobilization of lower castes in state politics picked up pace in the wake of the decline of the Congress after the fourth state elections and Charan Singh's estrangement from the grand old party. His purpose in forming the BKD was mainly to protect the interests of the rich peasantry, particularly the Jats and Yadavs of western UP, even though the party was projected as aiming to protect the interests of the entire peasant community. Although Charan Singh always identified himself with the interests of the *kisan*, he tried to subsume caste identities into a feeling of class (peasant) identity to give his outfit the flavour of a peasant movement.

His approach was partly dictated by his own caste background. Jats, who technically had to be classified as Shudras, occupied an intermediary position in state politics at that time. Their dominant caste status was often the root cause of their conflicts with lower castes. Charan Singh, therefore, had good reason to forge a *kisan* identity that the Jats would be leading, and to also promote an identity in opposition to town dwellers. This he did in order to transcend caste divisions and propagate a sense of peasant solidarity. Even though OBC leaders rallied around

Chaudhary Charan Singh, they soon realized that his scheme was not designed for the emancipation of their lot but was rather meant for the promotion of the interests of those who owned land. In fact, it was widely felt that the party's activities were likely to reinforce the Jat hegemony over the lower castes.

As revenue minister in charge of land reforms in Uttar Pradesh after Independence, Charan Singh had promoted the interests of what he called the middle peasantry by abolishing the *zamindari* system. The bulk of this class was to come from the intermediary castes, including his own—Jat.

Such an approach largely explains the peculiar character of UP, its lack of land reforms and Charan Singh's later conflicts with Nehru. In 1959, Charan Singh vigorously opposed the agricultural cooperatives project announced by Prime Minister Nehru in the Nagpur session of the Congress. He immediately published a book titled *Joint Farming X-rayed: The Problem and Its Solution*, in which he proposed a strategy of global development radically opposed to that of Nehru. In some ways, this book is the first manifesto of *kisan* politics in post-Independence India.

The Congress, meanwhile, didn't read the signs well, displaying keen shortsightedness in marginalizing Charan Singh in UP politics. Little did they realize that in the 1960s the social base of his *kisan* politics had taken on gigantic proportions. The Jats of western UP and Haryana grew wealthy, thanks to the increase in sugarcane production resulting from the extensive programmes in the framework of the Green Revolution. As these middle-level farmers asserted themselves, the overwhelming presence of Jats among them largely explained the growing success of Charan

Singh's politics in UP in the 1960s. In this way, Charan Singh was able to use caste as an important tool of political mobilization.

The BKD also tried to mobilize the backward castes by emphasizing their position in the caste hierarchy and their distinct economic interests, and on this basis claimed proportional representation for them in politics. It tried to identify the Congress party as the government that served the interests of the upper castes and industrialists. This rhetoric seemed to appeal to the backward classes as they saw the party as countering upper-caste dominance.

The Rise of the Socialists and Quota Politics

In Uttar Pradesh, socialist parties have also been instrumental in asserting caste identity for electoral gains. The 'rising star' of the Indian socialist movement, Dr Ram Manohar Lohia, a Baniya by caste, was probably the first person in the country who really incorporated caste as an ideology for mobilization. The socialists began to focus on the peasant's condition at a time when the Congress leadership was still rather urban-oriented. The founding conference of the Congress Socialist Party (CSP) was held in Patna in May 1934. It advocated the organization of peasants into '*kisan sanghs*'. The CSP broke away from the Congress in 1948, forming the Socialist Party, which eventually merged with Acharya Kripalani's Kisan Mazdoor Praja Party (KMPP) in 1953. The resultant outfit was called the Praja Socialist Party.

The PSP had done a lot for the mobilization of lower-caste peasants and workers in the Travancore–Cochin state when it was in power there. However, when his own government fired upon a group of agitating state workers, Lohia criticized it and asked for its resignation. He even advocated 60 per cent reservation for minorities, backward castes and SCs/STs in government services. Disagreeing with most of the PSP leaders, who were inclined to collaborate with the Congress, Lohia launched his own Socialist Party in 1956. Later, a laborious reunification process led to the founding of the Samyukta Socialist Party in 1964. Lohia remained at the helm of the SSP till his death in 1967.

Lohia was of the view that caste is the most overwhelming factor in the nation. Being of this view, he became one of the staunchest supporters of positive discrimination, or what he called 'unequal opportunities', not only in favour of the scheduled castes but also in favour of the backward castes. Lohia did not regard affirmative action in the education system as desirable but emphasized the need for quotas in administration and for electoral candidates. Obviously, reservations were intended to give a share of power to the lower castes and were viewed as an empowerment scheme. In 1959, the third national conference of the Socialist Party announced it was in favour of reserving at least 60 per cent of posts in the administration for OBCs. This demand was reiterated time and again in the fifth annual session of the party in 1961, as also in the first conference of the SSP in April 1966.

The socialists laid less emphasis on economic policy and harped more on two unrelated matters—language and backward castes. They urged that English be abolished forthwith and regional languages utilized solely, except for Hindi, which could be used as a link language. As mentioned before, they wished for a 60 per cent reservation in all government jobs and political seats for members of the backward and scheduled castes, and also for women. The socialists stood for the ending of economic disparities and abolishment of the caste system. They directed their appeal towards the rural areas and towards the lower and backward castes. It was, however, widely believed that the socialists sought the support of the middle agricultural classes, such as the Ahirs, from the 1960s onwards. These middle castes were generally tenants of Brahmins or Rajput *zamindars* in their villages but became landowners after the abolition of the *zamindari* system.

Apathy and Party Agendas Rule

With every new political regime and its chief minister—whether it was V.P. Singh, Mulayam Singh Yadav, Mayawati, Rajnath Singh, Akhilesh Yadav or the current man at the helm, Yogi Adityanath—increasingly more emphasis was placed on identity and communal politics rather than development in UP.

The worrying trend that began post-Independence and intensified after the dismal debacle of the Congress in 1967 has gone on unabated and with a ferocity that is scary. It was not without reason that UP witnessed the rise of some of the most powerful caste-based parties in the country from the 1980s onwards. The emergence of Mulayam Singh Yadav as a powerful Yadav leader, along with Kanshi Ram and his protégé Mayawati's BSP in the politics of Uttar Pradesh, was the outcome of a churning which, in many ways, started with the dilution of the Congress monopoly in the state. Though claims were made by subsequent governments of having brought about development in the state with amazing alacrity, the subtext has continued to be casteism and communalism. The result of this was that as the fake rant about development continued, UP continued to lag far behind many other parts of the country when it came to growth.

What perhaps characterized this succession of governments in the politics of Uttar Pradesh in post-Independence times was the tenure of chief ministers here. It was typical of UP politics that no chief minister was able to successfully complete five years in office until the BSP garnered a majority on its own in the 2007 assembly election and Mayawati got the distinction of being the first chief minister in the post-Independence history of Uttar Pradesh to have an uninterrupted five years in office. This speaks volumes of the plight of Uttar Pradesh right from the time of Independence.

For sure, the fortunes of the state began to change for the worse after Govind Ballabh Pant—the legendary freedom fighter, charismatic leader and first chief minister of UP—moved to the Centre to take charge as the country's home minister in December 1954. His departure was a turning point for the state as he had been in many ways the binding and unifying force not only for the grand old party to which he belonged but also for the state itself. His successor was Sampurnanand, who eventually had the longest run as chief minister of UP, from 28 December 1954 to 7 December 1960, but his tenure too was broken by assembly polls in April 1957. By the time Sampurnanand started his second innings in UP, the differences between Kamalapati Tripathi and Chandra Bhanu Gupta in the Congress had already reached a crisis point. Gupta emerged victorious in this battle and replaced Sampurnanand, but his uneasy ties with Indira Gandhi and his one-upmanship with Kamalapati Tripathi and Hemvati Nandan Bahuguna resulted in political instability. This led to the first non-Congress regime in UP, when Charan Singh became chief minister in 1967 for a brief period of ten months and twenty-two days.

From 1962 to 1967, UP politics was beset with a more acute kind of instability. In that span of just five years, the state saw three chief ministers who had very short tenures. This high drama continued throughout the 1970s. One after the other, the political regimes of Charan Singh, Tribhuvan Narain Singh, Hemvati Nandan Bahuguna, N.D. Tiwari, Ram Naresh Yadav and Babu Banarasi Das collapsed, with four spells of President's rule in between.

After the 1980 Congress victory at the Centre, Sanjay Gandhi picked Vishwanath Pratap Singh as the chief minister of UP, but Sanjay's death and Indira's insecurity around Bahuguna and others prompted another round of musical chairs. This resulted in Singh shifting to the Union cabinet in 1982. Sripati Mishra and N.D. Tiwari became chief ministers for short durations and left. In 1985, Prime Minister Rajiv Gandhi's personal preference was Vir Bahadur Singh (who was chief minister of UP from 24 September 1985 to 24 June 1988). But communal riots in Meerut and the political exigencies following the Bofors scandal forced Rajiv to draft Vir Bahadur into the Union cabinet. UP was handed over to Tiwari, who took the job for the third and last time.

In the early 1990s, UP entered the era of coalition politics, with BSP's Mayawati and SP's Mulayam Singh Yadav becoming the major players. This was a new phase in the history of UP, where power was sought by means of naked communal and caste polarization, and electoral algorithms were engineered by political leaders simply to retain office. The era saw the BJP cashing in on the Ram Janmabhoomi movement to seize power in UP, but its government was dismissed after the Babri Masjid demolition on 6 December 1992.

December 1993 saw the historic coming together of Mulayam Singh Yadav and Mayawati under a Kanshi Ram-supervised power-sharing formula. Mulayam Singh Yadav served as chief minister between 4 December 1993 and 3 June 1995. But the masterstroke of bringing together Dalits, minorities and backwards under one umbrella, which many saw as capable of changing the country's politics forever, proved short-lived. Personality clashes, caste antipathies and jostling ambitions led to ugly scenes on 2 June 1995, when halfway through his term Mulayam sought to break the alliance.

After its collapse, the BJP entered the scene, twice helping Mayawati to become chief minister. But her tenures too lasted for only brief periods of 184 days (21 March 1997 to 21 September 1997) and 483 days (3 May 2002 to 29 August 2003). In fact, it was during this period, in 1998, that UP got Jagdambika Pal heading it for just a day. The BJP's own rule between 1997 and 2002 saw Kalyan Singh, Ram Prakash Gupta and Rajnath Singh occupying the post of chief minister. This era of coalition politics finally ended with Mayawati's victory in the 2007 assembly election and a full term for her in office.

This picture of frequent creation and collapse of governments in UP is perhaps exceptional in the country. Despite being a highly politically significant state, UP did not see a single chief minister pull off a full term for more than fifty years. It is only since 2007 that three chief ministers—Mayawati, Akhilesh Yadav and Yogi Adityanath—have managed that feat. This paradox has been the irony of India's most populous state.

2

The Caste Crunch

In 2020, a twenty-year-old Dalit woman was gang-raped and murdered in Hathras, a city in the Brij region of what is known as the central or middle Doab geography of the state. The incident was extraordinary for its sheer brutality and violence. It was reported that the attackers strangulated the victim using her dupatta and that she was in a state of paralysis before she was murdered. It was alleged that the crime was committed by four men belonging to the powerful Thakur community. The incident shook the national conscience and there was all-round anxiety and concern for the safety of women in the most populous state of country. Outrage at the incident was expressed worldwide, from New York to Melbourne.

But, as things unfolded and Hathras came under intense scrutiny by the media, the issue of women's safety and security took a back seat. Instead, the case acquired a familiar caste angle. Media reports described the horrific crime as an outcome of the rivalry between the traditional upper-caste Thakurs and the Valmikis, now considered the opinion-maker Dalit community in the state. The ruling BJP regime now feared it would lose a significant chunk of its upper-caste vote bank if it succumbed to the demand for the conviction of all the accused Thakurs in the case. What aggravated matters for the party was that Yogi Adityanath, the person who headed the state, himself belonged to the Thakur community, and the perception that he represented the 'return of Thakurvad' in the state was very much alive in the political and social climate of Uttar Pradesh.

For the ruling BJP and its top leaders at the Centre, including Prime Minister Narendra Modi and Home Minister Amit Shah, Hathras was a very difficult political situation to handle. I see the BJP's immense electoral success since 2014 as having been on account of large sections of backward communities being attracted to the party's brand of Hindutva. In fact, this was a key achievement by Amit Shah the strategist, who was the general secretary in charge of the state in the 2014 election. This was the election that brought Modi to power with over 70 seats from UP, a phenomenal score for the BJP in the state. This was a massive showing by the BJP, resulting from Dalit support in combination with the party's existing upper-caste support. This combination continued to work in the 2017 assembly election and the 2019 Lok Sabha elections too. The Hathras incident and its handling, therefore, was a big setback for the BJP, both in Lucknow and in Delhi.

In fact, Hathras demonstrated very finely that politics in Uttar Pradesh is all about keeping the required caste equations in your favour. While other states in the country saw a dramatic transformation in the way politics was conducted in the post-reforms period, the land of the Ganga and Jamuna has continued to operate along the familiar lines of caste and community. So decisive has caste been in shaping the politics of the state over the years that it seems almost impossible to talk about any political development in UP without taking caste into consideration. A very interesting reminder of this stark reality of UP's social and political life is the practice of people announcing their caste identity—by means of stickers saying Yadav, Jat, Gurjar, Brahmin—on the windscreens of their vehicles. Though this is now banned by the state government, the very fact that the practice had been on for years reveals the influence caste has had on the social psyche of the people of the state.

That caste features in the day-to-day political and social affairs of the state is not a phenomenon that came about overnight. Its roots go back to the British Raj, for it was the British Indian government which, for the first time in Indian history, attempted to bring the complex and regionally diverse Indian society under a single system of common law. The sole purpose of the Raj was to construct social identities using an alien system of categorization along caste, religion and race, which served none but its own interests. The first caste-based census undertaken in 1931 in UP was very crucial in this regard. While the formal distinctions of caste were of little political significance in pre-colonial times, the census of 1931 introduced newer caste sensibilities across the Hindi heartland.

Building on the findings of this census, the Government of India Act 1935 incorporated a provision of reservation for what it termed as 'depressed classes'. In the same year, the British government classified different indigenous tribal groups under 'Schedule of Tribes'. One of the far-reaching implications of this classification was that, now more than ever, people began to identify themselves as Rajput, Brahmin, Bania and Muslim. Interestingly, it was around this period that the noted Hindi writer Munshi Premchand penned some of his finest and most powerful literary works on the caste conflicts between *zamindars*, Brahmins and Dalits.

But if newer sensibilities developing around caste were fuelling the literary imagination of writers like Premchand, they were simultaneously shaping the contours of national politics also. The clash between Gandhi and Ambedkar over the issue of a separate electorate for the 'depressed classes' was single-handedly responsible for making the politics of caste a national issue in British India. Gandhi strongly objected to the statutory separation of such classes from the Hindu fold and even went on to stage a fast against what he thought was a wicked conspiracy against Indian nationalism. It was broken only after Ambedkar agreed—in the famous Poona Pact—to reserved constituencies instead of separate electorates for the depressed classes.

One could endlessly debate the merits and demerits of Gandhi's and Ambedkar's approaches to caste, but it was evident that their concerns were largely guided by the sensibilities British India offered through initiatives like the caste-based census. It was indeed an irony that caste, which has impacted Indian politics so profoundly in post-Independence times, was made such a defining feature by the British empire.

The politics of Uttar Pradesh did not remain unaltered by this controversy. Though the Dalits in UP largely continued to sympathize with the Congress-led national movement after the historic Poona Pact, the community started to articulate its separate 'untouchable' identity also. Not just that, in several parts of the state, caste associations like Jatav Mahasabha emerged, which ultimately led to the formation of the Scheduled Castes Federation in UP. The growing appeal of this federation in UP indicated a shift away from the Congress and a closer identification with the politics Ambedkar championed. In fact, the federation famously invited Ambedkar to Lucknow to address a conference on 25 April 1948, where he appealed to the Scheduled Castes to unite as a political force. Needless to mention, the hallmark of the politics Ambedkar represented was the claim and assertion for political autonomy for the people who were then known as Scheduled Castes.

During the 1940s and '50s, caste distinctions and the question of adequate representation of different caste groups in Indian politics gained prominence like never before. The Congress leadership, which was involved in the series of negotiations with the British government over the possible future of India and its new Constitution, could not afford to overlook such concerns. On many occasions, Ambedkar, who by then had emerged as a champion of Dalit interests, took on the Congress leadership for not taking the issue of proportional representation for Scheduled Castes seriously. In 1944, the working committee of the All India Scheduled Castes Federation, under the leadership of Ambedkar, demanded that the Scheduled Castes should be recognized in the Constitution as a 'distinct and separate element' of the population, with proportional representation and separate electorates for representation in the central and provincial legislatures, and reservations in the Union and state executives, local governments and public services. The committee also criticized the Congress leadership's efforts to settle the communal problem between Hindus and Muslims through secret negotiations.

Finally, the Congress responded to such demands and criticism by offering Ambedkar a place in India's first cabinet, which was constituted right after the 1946 provincial elections. Ambedkar's federation had performed very poorly in the elections. It returned no candidate in Bombay, and it was in fact the Congress that won the bulk of Dalit seats in the 1946 elections. But he was given a place in the cabinet, with the responsibility of the law ministry. He was also the sole representative of the Scheduled Castes Federation in the newly elected Constituent Assembly of 296 members.

It was believed that the Congress leadership had tried to bring Ambedkar into the nationalist fold on the insistence of Gandhi. Ambedkar himself referred to the decision to take him into the cabinet as the greatest surprise of his life. Interestingly, the issue of his inclusion in the cabinet resurfaced decades later when, at an election rally in the capital in 2009, Mayawati accused the Congress of mistreating Ambedkar. In the same year, the BJP's former party president Lal Krishna Advani accused the Congress of not giving Ambedkar his due. Clearly, there was little truth in Mayawati's and Advani's claims, as the Congress had not only offered Ambedkar a place in the cabinet but had also ensured that he became a member, and then chairman, of the Constitution-drafting committee.

One could still argue that the Congress leadership was not quite generous in what it offered Ambedkar, but that it did not overlook him had profound implications for identity politics, which got constitutional validity and a base in India.

It was, after all, Ambedkar who submitted his book *States and Minorities: What Are Their Rights and How to Secure Them in the Constitution of Free India* to the Constituent Assembly's sub-committee on fundamental rights in 1947. This submission was highly influenced by the resolutions passed by the working committee of the All-India Scheduled Castes Federation in 1944, and proposed, almost along similar lines, an autonomous and distinct status for Scheduled Castes. The Constituent Assembly did not approve many of these proposals, but in part sixteen of the Constitution of India, 1950, 'special provisions for certain classes' were added, with the objective of ensuring 'protection and upliftment' of the Scheduled Classes. It was the scope and ambit of this clause that expanded in the post-Independence years to lead to the consolidation of quota politics.

Though caste very much existed in the social consciousness of the people, it did not, after Independence, straightaway become a mode of mobilizing the masses in the politics of Uttar Pradesh. The dominant position of the Congress in most of the states, including the Hindi-speaking ones such as UP and Bihar, did not allow *jati* to become an instrument of electoral gains. The party's upper-caste support base, coming mainly from the Rajputs of the state, and the remarkable influence the party's leaders from 'untouchable' communities enjoyed, kept the electoral prospects of other political parties in check. India's first prime minister, Jawaharlal Nehru, did not regard caste as a relevant category for state-sponsored social change either, and perhaps for this reason the Nehru government rejected the report of the First Backward Classes Commission appointed under the chairmanship of Kaka Kalelkar. Explaining the reason for this rejection, the home minister of the time, Govind Ballabh Pant, a Brahmin by caste, observed that recognition of the specified castes as backward might perpetuate the existing caste distinctions. The spectacular and emphatic majorities the Congress registered in the first three assembly elections held in UP only confirmed the electorate's faith in its leadership and its political programme.

But soon, growing factionalism in the party started paralysing the reputation it had earned for providing the successful foundation of competitive politics in India after Independence. The generational change in the political leadership of the state after the departure of Pant for the Centre in 1955 seemed to have created many factions within the party. Pant was the last of the prominent leaders of a national stature and a touch of charisma in UP who knew how to make enemies work together under him. But after his elevation to the central cabinet, the Congress in UP saw a struggle for control of the office of chief minister. This led to the formation of two broad groups in the party, the faction in power being called the 'ministerialist group' and the group out of power the 'dissident group'. In fact, the party 'high command' had to appoint three new chief ministers within a time span less than Pant's own tenure as CM.

There was also the caste angle to these factional rivalries. Though both the dissidents and the ministerialists each consisted of members of different castes, and both groups had members from the same castes, caste loyalties played a crucial role in the conflicts that emerged time and again within the party. Thus, when Dr Sampurnanand, a Kayastha, became chief minister of UP after Pant, he alienated some of his colleagues, who then formed a rival group under Chandra Bhanu Gupta. Gupta was a Bania and proved superior to Dr Sampurnanand in organizational ability and went on to become the chief minister after the resignation of Dr Sampurnanand. In 1965, Gupta too was challenged by a dissident, Kamalapati Tripathi, a Brahmin, who rallied his supporters to unseat Gupta. The role of these caste loyalties was in fact more dominant at the local level, since many of these state-level factions were tied together by district-level equations.

It is interesting to note that such factional conflicts in the Congress were not confined to the politics of Uttar Pradesh alone. The party faced similar crises in other states also, and there too, as in UP, it lacked leadership that had charisma and unchallenged authority. What made things worse for the Congress was the demise of its most charismatic leader, Jawaharlal Nehru, in 1964. His death created a vacuum in the political space that he had occupied for seventeen years since Independence. The Congress positioned Lal Bahadur Shastri as Nehru's successor, but he died under suspicious circumstances at Tashkent in 1966. With the death of two prime ministers in quick succession, the Congress party, which had previously been able to win constituencies based solely on the charisma of its leaders, could no longer do so.

The outcome of the historic 1967 elections was a wake-up call for the Congress, a reminder of the crises the party was facing both at the Centre and in the states. While the party managed to retain its power at the Centre with a reduced strength in the Lok Sabha under the leadership of Indira Gandhi, winning 283 seats compared to 361 in the previous election, it lost a significant chunk of votes to parties that had been on the electoral margins throughout the period of Congress dominance.

The politics of Uttar Pradesh too changed radically after the results of the 1967 election in the state. The Congress, for the first time since Independence, failed to secure an electoral majority, though it was still the single largest party in the Vidhan Sabha. The major beneficiaries of the party's slump in the state were the socialists and the Jana Sangh. The turning of their electoral fortunes was very significant, as they could now explore all possibilities to form a non-Congress coalition in the state.

The coalition idea appealed to all the parties that were opposed to the Congress, but in view of the serious ideological differences between the Jana Sangh and the others, they could not come together. But then, the historic split in the Congress over the election of Chandra Bhanu Gupta as leader of the Congress Legislative Party provided them the opportunity to rally around Chaudhary Charan Singh. Singh was annoyed with the party high command's choice of Gupta as its chief ministerial candidate and decided to leave, along with his confidant Jai Ram Verma and other MLAs, within a fortnight of Gupta being sworn in as chief minister. While Singh defended his decision as the most appropriate one for the future of the state, it was evident that he was more concerned about ousting the Congress from power. This anti-Congress sentiment finally brought the socialists, communists, Jana Sanghis, Republicans and independents together to form the SVD, which unanimously elected Charan Singh as their leader, as detailed in the previous chapter.

Charan Singh was sworn in as chief minister of the first coalition government in UP on 3 April 1967. Though there were clear ideological differences among the partners of the SVD, he tried hard to accommodate them in proportion to their strength in the ruling group. For the sustainability of the coalition, a common minimum programme was also formulated, avoiding the contentious issues. But the internal differences in the SVD soon became apparent. The leader of the Samyukta Socialist Party, Ram Manohar Lohia, threatened to withdraw from the SVD over the issue of land reforms. Many of the SVD partners were critical of the Jana Sangha for its use of the government machinery to spread its influence. Within months of the formation of the SVD, the anti-Congress euphoria appeared to have lost its edge and Charan Singh finally resigned on 17 February 1967, amid growing dissension within the ruling coalition.

The coalition of anti-Congress forces, consisting of many shades of socialists, the Jana Sangh, and the clumsy bunch of Swatantra Party leaders, was very short-lived. In fact, the fractured opposition enabled the Congress to come back to power in the 1969 election held after Charan Singh's resignation. Still, the implications of the 1967 election were far-reaching and decisive in how the politics of Uttar Pradesh unfolded thereafter. Never before in the politics of the state had parties propagating caste-based mobilization been in a position to bargain for power. Though the socialists, communists, Jana Sanghis and Republicans were very active on the political scene, they were not considered serious political contenders before the 1967 election. The rise of these forces on the political map of Uttar Pradesh was the result of the social and political churning that was going on among the different caste groups in the state.

The architects of this churning in Uttar Pradesh were leaders like Chaudhary Charan Singh and Ram Manohar Lohia, who had a firm base in their own communities. Singh went on to champion the cause of the middle-class farmers of north India, a class that emerged after the abolition of the *zamindari* system and the Green Revolution, in the name of peasantry. Lohia's name, on the other hand, became synonymous with quota politics, which he justified on the grounds that this would provide equal opportunities to lower and backward castes. The politics Singh and Lohia championed impacted the political scenario in UP decisively in the succeeding decades, when the state found itself divided mercilessly along caste and community lines. The caste blocks that emerged in the state were put to test by various political formations to build their own edifices.

3

The Growth and Growth of Caste

The outcome of the 1967 election was far-reaching in many significant ways in its impact on the politics of Uttar Pradesh. The coalition of anti-Congress forces, consisting of many shades of socialists, the Bharatiya Jana Sangh and the Swatantra Party leaders, appeared to scatter away in the states where they had formed governments in 1967. But the Congress split in December 1969 seemed to bolster the Lohiaite strategy (of all-out unity against Indira's Congress) even after Lohia's death in October 1967, leading to the grand alliance of all the anti-Congress parties (barring the two left parties) in the 1971 general election. But then, the results of the general election showed that these parties had lost the confidence of the people. The alliance was routed across the country, except in Gujarat and Tamil Nadu.

The most populous state of the country, meanwhile, was being worked by various political formations to build their own empires. In a span of just five years, the state witnessed the brief tenures of Charan Singh, Tribhuvan Narain Singh, Kamalapati Tripathi, Hemwati Nandan Bahuguna and, finally, N.D. Tiwari.

While Charan Singh was a Jat CM, Tribhuvan Narain Singh was a Thakur and Kamalapati Tripathi a Brahmin. The ascendancy of Bahuguna, a Garhwali Brahmin, and his successor Tiwari, a Kumaoni Brahmin, further confirmed the hold of Brahmins in the leadership of the Congress as well as in the politics of the state.

The instability and turbulence that marked the politics of Uttar Pradesh amidst the rise of new forces on the political map of the state did not end even after the Janata Party's historic win in the 1977 general election. Despite the party's thumping majority in the state assembly, a fight broke out between the Chandrashekhar and Charan Singh–Madhu Limaye groups over who would be the chief ministerial candidate. Chandrashekhar wanted Ram Dhan, a Dalit MP from Lalganj (Azamgarh), to be sworn in as chief minister, but finally Ram Naresh Yadav, the MP from Azamgarh, was voted by the MLAs as their leader. The government lasted for almost two years, but Yadav had to resign in the wake of the infamous Narayanpur (Deoria) case of police atrocities. He was succeeded in February 1979 by Banarasi Das, a leader of the Vaishya community, who in turn was sacked by Indira Gandhi, who came into power in 1980 after the failure of what was termed as the Janata experiment.

But the fate of Uttar Pradesh continued to deteriorate. With Vishwanath Pratap Singh—a close aide of Indira Gandhi and the raja of Manda in Allahabad—ascending to power in Uttar Pradesh, the law-and-order problem in the state reached unprecedented levels. During Singh's government there were allegations of fake police encounters, including the Behmai massacre of 1981, in which twenty Rajputs were killed by the bandit Phoolan Devi. After dacoits killed his brother, Justice Chandrashekhar Pratap

Singh, in 1982, Singh resigned. He was replaced by Shripati Mishra, a Sultanpur Brahmin. Mishra, too, was removed in 1984, and N.D. Tiwari got his second shot at chief ministership. Tiwari led the Congress to victory in the election held months after Indira's assassination. However, Rajiv Gandhi, remaining true to the Congress culture of clipping the wings of regional leaders, replaced him with the Gorakhpur Thakur Vir Bahadur Singh within months. Singh was chief minister from September 1985 to June 1988, when Tiwari returned. But the Congress under Tiwari suffered a historic defeat in 1989 and has struggled in the state ever since.

Amid these splits, mergers and collapse of the Congress, three parties—the BJP, BSP and SP—surged, both electorally and organizationally, in UP. The defeat of the Congress in the 1989 Lok Sabha election was a big moment in the politics of the country. The ouster of the grand old party from power owed to the strategic failure of Prime Minister Rajiv Gandhi and his counterpart in Uttar Pradesh, N.D. Tiwari, who tacitly approved the *shilanyaas* ceremony in Ayodhya, orchestrated by the Vishwa Hindu Parishad (VHP), in the hope of winning Hindu votes. As it turned out, the move proved suicidal for the Congress. V.P. Singh became the prime minister of the National Front government, comprising his Jan Morcha and the Janata Dal, with the BJP and left parties playing a supportive role.

The V.P. Singh wave also brought a turnaround for the opposition in UP, where the Janata Dal emerged as the single largest party in the assembly election held in the same year. The rise of Kanshi Ram's BSP in the state was equally surprising for many political observers of the time. But the person to benefit the most from the election was Mulayam Singh Yadav, who pulled off a strategic alliance with the Janata Dal and went on to become chief minister of UP. But again, the collapse of the V.P. Singh government at the Centre in less than a year of its coming to power forced Mulayam Singh to seek the support of Chandrashekhar's Janata Dal so he could continue in office with the backing of the Congress. It was during this tenure as chief minister that Mulayam Singh Yadav ordered police firing on kar sevaks marching to Ayodhya in October 1990. But then, the reverberations from the Centre were again felt in Lucknow in 1991, when Mulayam Singh Yadav had to resign after the Congress withdrew its support to the Chandrashekhar government. The mid-term election that followed in Uttar Pradesh came as a shock to Yadav as his party could win only 30 seats, and the BJP, riding the Hindutva wave with slogans like '*Ram lala hum aaenge, mandir waheen banaaenge*', surged to power with a comfortable majority in the state assembly.

In 1991, Kalyan Singh became the chief minister of Uttar Pradesh. He was a strong Lodh (a backward community) leader of the BJP and a robust face of the Ram Mandir movement. But the Kalyan Singh government was dismissed after the Babri Masjid demolition of 6 December 1992, an event that really shook the nation and whose ramifications can be felt to date.

This was a phase in UP politics that left a deep impression on my mind. Those were perhaps the most tumultuous years in UP politics, and I was to understand only years later what those years meant and how their impact was to play out for decades to come. The mood that pervaded the air those days is palpable to me even today. Young people like me had witnessed the kar sevaks walking in their hundreds across the streets of Lucknow, mainly from Charbagh railway station, going down the station road where I stayed, to eventually board the vehicles organized for them to get to Ayodhya. It was therefore unimaginable that after all this the BJP would not come back to power whenever the next state elections happened in Uttar Pradesh.

But the BJP underperformed against its own 1991 showing of 221 seats, winning only 177 in the state assembly in 1993. And this was because of the rise of two politicians who would eventually take turns to rule the state for many years. While the BJP could not get the majority numbers, the man who would become a political force, Kanshi Ram, turned the game on its head. Kanshi Ram and his protégé Mayawati formed an alliance with Mulayam Singh Yadav, and were supported by like-minded parties in forming a government in the name of secularism in UP. So, even in the post-Babri-demolition scenario, the BJP, despite being the single largest party in the assembly, could not come to power.

But the secular alliance, with its enormous governance and personality clashes, did not last. With Mulayam Singh Yadav as chief minister, the combination ruled the state for only eighteen months. It was clear that this was a caste combination that was being experimented with. The twin themes of caste, with the rise of Mulayam, and the mandir agenda of the BJP left no space for anything like development.

The impact of the 'secular' experiment in UP was definitely not limited to Lucknow. The BJP and Sangh strategists figured that the party needed more than its core Hindutva agenda to come to power at the Centre.

The year 1995 became another one of upheaval in politics in both Lucknow and Delhi. By this time, I had become a journalist, a young reporter beginning to understand a little of what all this meant. Clearly perceiving the need to build a larger coalition, BJP strategists went to the acceptable face of their politics at the time. In November 1995, during the BJP national session in Mumbai, Lal Krishna Advani himself declared the moderate Atal Bihari Vajpayee as the BJP's prime ministerial face for the future.

Back home in Lucknow, nothing was going right in the alliance between Mulayam Singh Yadav and Mayawati. The ugliest turn came when on 2 June 1995, at a state guest house, Mayawati accused Mulayam Singh and his men of trying to kill her.[6] She had to lock herself inside a room at Mirabai Marg, Lucknow, when some SP workers allegedly tried to molest her.

By then, two new key players had emerged on the scene to form a new alliance, leaving Mulayam Singh Yadav out. Murli Manohar Joshi, a hardline face of the Ram Mandir movement, and businessman-turned-Rajya Sabha MP Jayant Malhotra from Kanpur were bringing together the BJP and Mayawati.

Back in Delhi, when Mayawati visited Advani at his house, many reporters like me had only one question to ask the latter: 'Have you forgotten the past; have you buried the past?' This was because Mayawati was an ally of Mulayam Singh Yadav, whom the BJP had accused of killing innocent kar sevaks. But such questions were ignored. The BJP chose to make Mayawati

India's first Dalit woman chief minister. Amidst all this, the prominent RSS ideologue K.N. Govindacharya had remarked that Vajpayee (as BJP's prime ministerial choice) was simply a '*mukhauta*', implying that it was Advani calling the shots in the party. This, naturally, did not go down well with Vajpayee, who was then on the threshold of creating a 'new-look' BJP, which eventually meant a coalition called the National Democratic Alliance and a government at the Centre that lasted for over six years, after an initial thirteen-day fiasco in 1996 of a Vajpayee-led government. This six-year government was one that I tracked and reported on closely.

With Vajpayee's charisma, charm and universal appeal working fairly well across all coalition partners, the BJP-led NDA government successfully completed a full five-year term in office in 2004. But the fortunes of Uttar Pradesh kept swinging between mergers and splits that the BJP, BSP and SP played with throughout this period. Curiously, for many observers like me, the BSP and SP ascended to power on their own in the state while making inroads into a significant portion of the upper-caste vote bank. The strategy of social engineering, as it was called, rewarded the BSP with decent majority numbers in 2007 (206 seats in a 403-member Vidhan Sabha); the SP too surged to power in 2012 with 224 seats, with young Akhilesh Yadav successfully giving the party an image makeover.

Then came the year 2014, when the BJP registered its biggest ever victory in Uttar Pradesh in the Lok Sabha elections (winning 71 out of the 80 seats in the state) as a result of the combined efforts of party strategist Amit Shah and its prime ministerial face

Narendra Modi. Though the party championed the politics of development, what actually worked for it on the ground were the caste calculations done by it in the wake of Modi's rising popularity in the state. During the election, my visits to Modi's constituency of Varanasi and to the eastern and central regions of the state gave me a fine first-hand sense of how the BJP reached out to other backward castes in the state and brought them into the Hindutva fold through its Samajik Nyaya Sammelans and other similar campaigns. This was the strategy that led to the Modi storm in which the SP, BSP and Congress lost their traditional voters to the BJP like never before. The trend only gained consistency, as was evident when the BJP won the 2017 assembly election in UP and the 2019 general election with massive margins.

From Mulayam Singh Yadav to Mayawati, and then to Yogi Adityanath—I have witnessed some of the most transformative phases of UP politics and have been left alternately curious and shocked at the political developments. While the unpredictability of UP politics left me puzzled and often defied conventional wisdom, I could clearly see UP taking a decisive 'caste' turn in the post-Babri-demolition period. The obvious outcome of this turn was that caste combinations continued to endure, rattling the fortunes of UP for years to come.

4

Collapse of the Congress

It was a cold and dull winter's day—18 December 2020—that I saw Congress leaders trooping into 10 Janpath in Delhi, easily the most famous address of the party, for an equally cheerless meeting. That meeting at Sonia Gandhi's residence did not convey a pleasant picture of the party at all. Since the defeat of the Congress in 2014, meetings such as this one had become part of the party's culture of introspection but had led to no major organizational reforms.

This meeting was in response to a dissident letter that twenty-three Congress leaders, including MPs and former ministers, had written five months ago demanding more visible and active leadership. It was a move that was seen as an attempt to challenge the leadership of the party's interim chief, Sonia Gandhi. While the meeting was attended by both the dissenters—Ghulam Nabi Azad, Anand Sharma, Bhupinder Singh Hooda, Shashi Tharoor, Manish Tewari, Prithviraj Chavan—and the loyalists—such as A.K. Antony, Ashok Gehlot, Kamal Nath and Ambika Soni—it did not result in anything substantial. In fact, the oldest party of the world's largest democracy again found itself in a familiar dilemma—it was unhappy over the leadership of the Gandhi family, yet it could not look beyond the Gandhis for leadership.

Most observers saw its current plight as part of the larger crisis the Congress had been facing ever since it slumped to its lowest-ever tally of 44 in the 2014 general election. The Modi victory had flattened the Congress, both strategically and ideologically, in this historic election. And the party which once enjoyed a remarkable support base in urban as well as rural India was now forced to face a huge embarrassment.

The tug of war between Sonia Gandhi's old guard and Rahul Gandhi now revealed the party's organizational failures too. In politics, a leader's overall popularity and acceptance are also judged by how he or she performs in his or her home turf, and not just by how the person helms the party. We often see leaders contesting the same election from two different constituencies, perhaps actually revealing that they don't have much faith in their winnability.

When I was out on my journey of nearly three months for the digital reportage series 'From UP for UP' during the 2019 Lok Sabha election, it was clear that I had to visit Amethi. There was already talk that an outsider like Smriti Irani could turn the tables there. Another reason for the visit was to ascertain whether Amethi had become so shaky for Rahul Gandhi that he had to contest from Wayanad in Kerala too. So, Amethi was an important visit for me. As I travelled across the constituency, the first political complaint about Rahul Gandhi from the people was that he was hardly seen there. At best he could be seen waving to them from inside his vehicle. In contrast, Smriti Irani, an actual outsider, had spent days and months among the people of

Amethi, housing herself there to create a strong political challenge for Rahul Gandhi. Speaking to people in the small main market area of Amethi, I discovered that those loyal to the Gandhis were still not ready to give Smriti Irani any chance. The youths I spoke to in the market straightaway demanded to know where Rahul Gandhi was. And with this I got the first clear message that Rahul Gandhi was in trouble in Amethi itself, one of the strongest Gandhi family seats ever. I reported all this, predicting Smriti Irani's victory in Amethi, for which I was widely acclaimed as the only journalist to say that Rahul Gandhi's days as the Amethi MP were over.

There was a time when the Congress dominated Uttar Pradesh and had remarkable popularity and reach among all sections of society. Its legacy as a party that had fought for India's independence, and the league of charismatic leaders it produced, kept the electoral prospects of all opposition parties at bay. Those were the days when Brahmins as well as Muslims and Dalits showed relentless faith in the party as the only entity that could turn around the fortunes of millions and millions of people. Much of the loyalty the party enjoyed across different constituencies in UP owed to its strong organizational base in the state. Adding immensely to its popularity among the masses was the touch of charisma some of its stalwarts had—notable among them being Pandit Govind Ballabh Pant, the first chief minister of Uttar Pradesh.

Pandit Pant, a very close aide of Jawaharlal Nehru's, played an instrumental role in keeping the UP Congress united after Independence. Widely hailed as a genius of organization, Pandit Pant had the unique ability of running the affairs of the state without any personal following in the factional sense. Often, in matters of conflict, he managed to bring about a consensus through his fine and brilliant sense of judgement, leaving hardly anyone dissatisfied. His presence in the state capital, Lucknow, therefore kept the UP Congress intact, despite several internal issues and conflicts that beset it.

How important Pandit Pant was for the unity of the UP Congress soon became clear. After completing a brief tenure of barely two and half years as CM, he was elevated to the Centre by Prime Minister Jawaharlal Nehru in December 1954, a decision that led to much hue and cry among the party members at the time. It was feared that his departure would be followed by a power tussle for the post of chief minister in UP. This did not happen immediately, though, as the two key rival groups operating in the party, one led by Chandra Bhanu Gupta and the other by Mohan Lal Gautam, unanimously agreed on the name of Dr Sampurnanand, senior Congressman and the state's home minister, who in many ways was a natural successor to Pandit Pant.

But in a span of just four years, the UP Congress found itself in an unprecedented crisis when a group of dissenters led by Algu Rai Shastri demanded Dr Sampurnanand's resignation, alleging that administration in UP had deteriorated under his rule and that he had split the party into two. So serious was the crisis that the party high command in New Delhi had to intervene and settle the crisis, which, however, left the UP Congress divided into even more factions. Such crises thus kept surfacing in the party in the succeeding years and often required intervention by New Delhi to settle. One of the reasons why internal dissension increasingly rattled the UP Congress in Dr Sampurnanand's time was that he lacked the organizational skills and charisma his predecessor Pandit Pant had. Though Dr Sampurnanand commanded the same universal respect as Pandit Pant in party circles, he had to largely depend on the backing of the faction leaders who commanded their own following within the party and who lobbied for their own cause, leaving the organization in disarray. Many of them had considerable influence in their caste constituencies, making their handling very tricky for the state leadership.

These were the first signs of what was often referred to as the 'syndicate culture' in the Congress, where different party leaders form their own syndicates or groups owing to their influence in particular caste constituencies and bargain with the state or central leadership for lucrative positions. This impacted the Uttar Pradesh Congress most, as it was in the electoral politics of UP among all states that caste mattered most too. It was a factor that now single-handedly decided the fate of all political parties.

It is interesting to note that with the rise of Mandal and Kamandal politics in the 1990s, these big caste leaders of the Congress decisively lost a major chunk of their support base to leaders like Mayawati and Mulayam Singh Yadav. Still, the party could not shrug off its syndicate culture, and to this day it hasn't. This is the perspective from which one should view Jitin Prasada, an old-time Congressman who joined the BJP in June 2021, accusing the Congress of ignoring the Brahmins in Uttar Pradesh. If some political observers are to be believed, his ouster from the Congress was engineered by the BJP to woo the Brahmin vote bank for the 2022 assembly election, but in my opinion the move was more to do with his own political survival as he had lost his appeal and support base over the years among the Brahmins of the region and was in no position to influence them. This has been the problem for the grand old party post the 1990s: to date, it finds itself divided into factions—old vs new, Brahmin vs Thakur—despite the fact that the majority of its leaders no longer have appeal among the masses.

Factionalism within the Uttar Pradesh Congress, which started during Dr Sampurnanand's tenure, only intensified in the 1960s and 1970s, with many leaders of rival caste groups replacing each other as chief minister of Uttar Pradesh, one after the other. When Dr Sampurnanand completed his second tenure as chief minister in December 1960, a political crisis reared its head again, this time led by Kamalapati Tripathi and Chandra Bhanu Gupta. This culminated in Dr Sampurnanand's shift to the Jaipur Raj Bhawan, where he served as governor of Rajasthan till 1967. The fact that a leader of his stature was forced to leave Lucknow spoke volumes about the internal politics of the UP Congress. When the powerful Congress stalwart Chandra Bhanu Gupta succeeded Sampurnanand, the UP Congress entered a fresh phase of turbulence, which saw some extraordinary developments that eventually changed the face of not only UP politics but the very country's politics.

One of the fallouts was that all state Congress leaders holding ministerial office, including Chandra Bhanu Gupta, were asked to resign and join party work under the famous Kamaraj Plan. Gupta, known for his strong following in the state unit but also for his uneasy ties with New Delhi, and specially with Indira Gandhi, was forced to resign in 1963, but made a comeback after the 1967 Lok Sabha and assembly elections, where the Congress, for the first time after Independence, lost the major chunk of its support base to socialists and Jana Sanghis. The year 1967 saw the Congress running an eighteen-day government in Uttar Pradesh under the leadership of Gupta, but finally losing to Chaudhary Charan Singh, who revolted from the party and formed the first non-Congress coalition government in the state. This first coalition government in UP could last for only ten months, but it brought the crisis in the Congress to the fore, the dents in its dominance now clear for all to see.

These were also the days when the fate of Uttar Pradesh was linked to New Delhi. The state supplied 85 seats to the Lok Sabha; this being so, a hold over its politics was considered key for any political party wishing to ascend to power at the Centre. The transition and turbulences in New Delhi, in turn, impacted UP affairs directly too. Between 1963 and 1970, the central leadership of the Congress was also going through a phase of huge transformation. After the death of Jawaharlal Nehru and Lal Bahadur Shastri, Indira Gandhi was chosen to be the prime minister of India in 1966. This led to a huge upheaval in the grand old party, as there were already rifts between the party's organizational bosses and Indira Gandhi, the executive head, over plans for the revival of the party and its future course of action after its poor showing in the 1967 general election.

These rifts took a decisive turn in the 1969 Bangalore session of the All India Congress Committee (AICC) over the party's choice of presidential candidate. The Syndicate, a powerful grouping of leaders within the Congress, nominated N. Sanjiva Reddy as the official candidate of the party while Indira Gandhi supported then Vice President V.V. Giri. With the clear victory of Giri, Indira Gandhi was expelled from the party, and a split in the Congress now became inevitable. It led to the formation of Indira Gandhi's New Congress or Congress (R), while the unit with the Syndicate leaders became Congress (O). This splitting of the Congress party into two was one of the biggest developments of post-Independence times in India and formally the beginning of what is called the Indira era in Indian politics.

The politics of the Hindi heartland became the object of these developments almost immediately. The new government in Uttar Pradesh, formed after the 1969 mid-assembly election, disintegrated naturally after the Congress split, and in an attempt to curtail the old block of the Congress, Indira Gandhi even went on to support the Charan Singh-led Bhartiya Kranti Dal to make him the chief minister of the state, though only for a very short period of eight months in 1970. This was purely a tactical move, largely orchestrated to absorb the BKD into the new Congress. But when attempts to crack the BKD failed, Charan Singh was asked to resign by governor B. Gopala Reddi.[7] Of course Singh would not resign, and in an extraordinary move in the same year, the Centre imposed President's rule in UP just before the state assembly was to convene.

Clearly, here the old and new blocks of the Congress were playing Uttar Pradesh for their own interests. Indira Gandhi was doing everything to consolidate the position of her new party, and all her political moves were carefully planned to sideline the Congress (O) faction of the 'old Turks'. Finally, with a landslide victory in the 1971 general election, she got the decisive upper hand over this faction, and here began the era of her dominance.

This was also the time for Indira Gandhi to take charge of political affairs in Lucknow in a much more commanding way. The caste factions in the UP Congress were still in operation, and now they had to be dealt with in keeping with the dynamics of the new Congress. The strategies for governing the most populous state of the country were worked out by the 'high command' in New Delhi.

The dilemma of choosing the right chief minister for UP continued to destabilize matters in UP, and New Delhi imposed President's rule in the state several times, despite the fact that the party had a stable majority in the 425-member assembly. For example, when Hemwati Nandan Bahuguna resigned in November 1975, President's rule was imposed, despite the party being in a clear majority in the assembly. President's rule was imposed four times in Uttar Pradesh in a span of just ten years, between 1970 and 1980, clearly indicating that the Congress high command in New Delhi did not find state leaders capable of running the government. Often, it sent leaders from New Delhi who could remain loyal in tricky situations.

This 'high command' culture in the party was carried to new levels in the post-Emergency era, when the Congress and Indira Gandhi made a comeback in the 1980s after the failed Janata Party experiment. The central leadership of the party appointed state chief ministers according to their own political preference, also summoning them back to New Delhi as and when they wished to. That was how V.P. Singh became chief minister of Uttar Pradesh in 1980 and found himself sent back to New Delhi after only two years. This trend continued into the time of Rajiv Gandhi, who became the prime minister after Indira

Gandhi's assassination. He chose Vir Bahadur Singh to head the government in Uttar Pradesh in 1985, but recalled him to New Delhi in 1988, passing on the baton to N.D. Tiwari, the last chief minister from the Congress in Uttar Pradesh, who held office till 1989.

By this time the Congress was already seeing dents in its support base, but during the 1990s it saw the most decisive challenge to its authority, in both the state as well as the Centre, from parties that were realigning the political equations in UP in the name of backward-caste politics. Leaders like Mulayam Singh Yadav and Mayawati were now the new power players in UP politics. The rise of communal politics, which the BJP represented in the state in the name of Lord Ram, was another challenge to the grand old party. Riding on caste and communal appeal, these parties made inroads into communities that had traditionally belonged to the Congress. The party was in no position to counter this strategy, and by that time its remarkable organizational unity was already in disarray and its affairs were tightly controlled by the party high command sitting in New Delhi.

So close were the state heads of the Congress to the high command that this was joked about in political circles. One of the tallest upper-caste leaders of the Congress in UP was N.D. Tiwari. Nirmal Pathak, a senior journalist who covered Congress politics for years, once discovered that he was often called New Delhi Tiwari in political circles. The political play of leaders like him was to control Lucknow by means of machinations in Delhi, made possible by their closeness to the central leadership. This is the problem that has plagued the party for decades now, if we look at the Congress's shaky relationship with the state since

1989. Another factor was that the party's regional leaders no longer enjoyed the authority or charisma they once did among the masses. The SP, BSP and BJP were the beneficiaries of the Congress decline, and they turned around their political fortunes largely cashing on this.

During the time of the power tussle between the SP, BSP and BJP in Lucknow of the past couple of decades, the Congress had already lost its dominant position in the state. It was very much present and active on the political front, but more in the role of a coalition partner. Witnessing the politics of UP in the post-Babri-demolition period always reminded me of how the Congress lost its ground in UP and how Rajiv Gandhi's strategy of winning the Hindu sentiment by opening the gates of the disputed Ram Janmabhoomi–Babri Masjid structure in 1985 ultimately went against it. During my visits to different parts of the state over the last two decades, many Congress strategists have acknowledged the failure of Gandhi's move, but also explained that he had to respond to the communal and caste politics of the time. There was definitely some truth in their explanation. However, they tend to forget that the tactic of polarization in the state was actually introduced by the SP, BSP and BJP to counter Congress dominance in the state. By falling into the trap of the VHP, Rajiv Gandhi only provided the opportunity the BJP was seeking after its rout in the 1984 general election.

Despite having been shunted to the margins in UP since 1989, there was a phase when the Congress looked up in the state, but it completely failed to capitalize on this. The rise of the SP, BSP and BJP meant that these parties managed to create a strong political workforce in the state and the Congress kept on losing its cadres to these parties. Still, the positive image of the Manmohan Singh government at the Centre helped the party win 22 seats in 2007. Some of them were remarkable first-time victories, such as that of cricketer Mohammad Azharuddin in Moradabad.

Very quickly, a debate began as to whether this good showing had opened a road to recovery for the Congress in the state. But with the party failing to capitalize on it or show greater interest in consolidating its gains, despite improving its tally to 28 in the 2012 assembly election, this good phase fizzled out as fast as it had come. In 2017, it was reduced to just 7 seats in the Vidhan Sabha, its worst ever performance in the state.

5

The Caste-based Criminal Gangs of UP

If there is a recent incident that epitomizes the caste–politics–crime nexus in Uttar Pradesh, it is the encounter killing of gangster Vikas Dubey in 2020 and the questionable conduct of the UP police. His encounter killing created an uproar because of the extremely suspicious circumstances of his elimination—why was he killed after he had been arrested in Ujjain? Was there a fear that on reaching Lucknow and on being interrogated he would spill the beans on the larger criminal–politician nexus that had endured in UP for decades?

On the dawn of 10 July 2020, Uttar Pradesh—and indeed the entire nation—was hooked to the news as the melodramatic and dreadful end to what looked like a perfect script for a Bollywood crime thriller from the 1970s unfolded. As news broke of the encounter killing of Vikas Dubey, a history-sheeter accused of killing eight policemen in Bikru village, people were glued to their TV screens to learn the exact sequence of events that led to his being gunned down. It was reported that Dubey was trying to flee from police custody while he was being taken to Kanpur from Ujjain in Madhya Pradesh, where he had been arrested the previous day at Mahakal temple. Apparently, he managed to snatch a pistol from a police officer after the police vehicle carrying him lost control and even fired at the police team before being shot dead by the police in retaliation.

Not everyone, however, found this story convincing. Some of the journalists who were trailing the police convoy questioned this narrative—as did former UP chief minister Akhilesh Yadav. The way Dubey and his accomplices had killed eight police personnel in cold blood on 3 July 2020 and were chased by the police in a highly melodramatic hide-and-seek game, followed by another round of blood and horror, would have made for a powerful script for any filmmaker.

As a long-time observer of UP politics, I too could see the cinematic potential in this drama, which took nearly a week to unfold on TV and in the newspapers. For me, however, the saga of Vikas Dubey was not just about the nexus of crime and politics in UP. It was in fact the angle of caste that made this incident particularly revealing of the politics of Uttar Pradesh. The reactions to this killing on social media perhaps aptly captured this. For many, Dubey was not just a gangster but a Brahmin, a tiger who commanded the love and respect of the community. Some even saw the episode as illustrative of a turf war between the Brahmins and Thakurs in UP, as it took place under the government of a Thakur chief minister, Yogi Adityanath, they held.[8]

It is typical of the caste-based crime scenario in UP that Vikas Dubey's encounter upset the Brahmins, creating a socio-political perception that Brahmins were being targeted by the current regime in UP. This is the kind of politics that obtains in Uttar Pradesh. In my view, despite the questionable manner in which Vikas Dubey was killed, he was, after all, a hardened criminal and not worthy of any Brahmin backlash of the kind one saw. But that's the irony of local equations in UP's political demographics.

An outsider might find such a narrative amusing, but those who know Uttar Pradesh will immediately understand the background to this narrative. In UP, after all, gang wars are essentially caste wars, and the reality has not yet changed despite a considerable decline in serious crime in the state. Not long ago, UP was in the headlines for the murder of one of its mafia dons, Munna Bajrangi, a Rajput and a gangster-turned-politician from the Purvanchal region of the state. Bajrangi, known as a close aide of Mukhtar Ansari, another influential don-turned-politician from the Mau region, was reportedly gunned down by one of his rivals, Sunil Rathi, on 9 July 2018, just before he was to be produced in court for his involvement in the murder of BJP leader Krishnanand Rai.

Interestingly, it was the sensational murder of Rai, a Bhumihar Brahmin and MLA from the Mohammadabad constituency of Ghazipur, that made Bajrangi an iconic figure of eastern UP in 2005. Rai had ascended in politics with the support of another gangster, Brajesh Singh, who had already been running his syndicate in the region. But from the 1990s, Ansari's rise started to pose a serious challenge to Singh's monopoly over coal and railway contracts. By that time Bajrangi had already gained notoriety for killing BJP leader Rajkumar Singh in Rampur in 1996, and it was also some time during this period that he aligned with Ansari, who used him to counter his rival Brajesh Singh while he himself focused on pursuing a career in active politics. In many ways, Rai's murder in 2005 was the 'high point' of the Ansari-vs-Singh rivalry in the state. The talking point of the murder was Bajrangi and his men who, according to media reports, fired almost 400 rounds of bullets from their six AK-47 rifles in broad daylight on Rai. Ironically, it was Munna Bajrangi who introduced the AK-47 to the gangs of UP and made this deadly weapon a symbol of power and dominance in the state. This was also the time of transition from the country-made pistol—the *katta*—to Russian rifles like the AK-47 in the UP underworld.

Many of these stories about the Bajrangis, Dubeys, Ansaris, Tiwaris, Shahis, Shuklas and Yadavs have come under the spotlight for the fascinating glimpses they provide into the crime syndicates of Uttar Pradesh. Political parties at different points of time hired these gangsters to hone their caste interests; and gangsters shifted their loyalties across political parties and themselves turned into full-time politicians. All this makes for the fascinating story of UP as a hub of organized crime that percolated into its politics too.

But the state did not acquire the notoriety of a 'Chicago of the East' overnight. Its roots go back to the 1950s and '60s, when Gorakhpur University became a battleground between two dominant castes of the region—the Thakurs and the Brahmins. Those were the days when control of the governing body of a university offered enormous opportunities to influence numerous highly desirable appointments. It was over this issue that the interests of S.N.M. Tripathi, the Gorakhpur district magistrate and founder-president of the university, also known as Pandit Tripathi in the region, started clashing with those of Mahant Digvijaynath, a Thakur who was a governing committee member of the university. Tripathi saw Mahant's proposal of merging his Maharana Pratap Degree College into the university as a threat to his dominance in the affairs of the university, and soon both sides began to recruit muscle power. This was just the beginning of caste-based gangsterism in eastern UP.

By the 1970s, student politics had become highly influential in the north Indian states and Uttar Pradesh was no exception. The campus of Gorakhpur University too saw the rise of many student leaders who supplied muscle power to their political bosses. One of them was Harishankar Tiwari, a Brahmin, who was often used by Pandit Tripathi to counter the influence of the Thakurs on the campus. Tiwari, a postgraduate in sociology from the university, soon became a small-time contractor and rose to power in the region under Tripathi's patronage. His name became almost synonymous with property and land deals, and no one dared to bypass him.

Tiwari, in more than one way, was the first prominent mafia-man-turned-politician in the state. He was ready to help any political party and was also sought after by parties. There is one story that speaks volumes of Tiwari's clout in his area. Vir Bahadur Singh, the dominant Thakur chief minister from the Congress, was from Gorakhpur and was at loggerheads with the mafia whom he wanted to subdue. Eastern UP was also among the poorest regions of Uttar Pradesh, and Singh attempted to industrialize the area. But Harishankar Tiwari notoriously sought protection money from employees of the Bajaj group while they were doing a survey near Gorakhpur for a scooter factory to be set up. This is just one example of how efforts to industrialize the region failed even in the 1980s, despite a chief minister himself pushing for it. Such was the deep-rooted malice of the mafia in eastern UP.

Tiwari's rise in Purvanchal, however, did not go unchallenged. The first serious challenge to his dominance came from adjoining Basti district. Virendra Pratap Shahi, a fellow student leader and a close aide of Ram Kinkar Singh, ex-MLA of Basti, started as a middleman for government contracts in Basti but shifted to Gorakhpur after falling out with Ram Kinkar Singh over some personal issues in the late 1970s.

In Gorakhpur, the Brahmins and Thakurs were already at loggerheads with each other, and on 27 August 1979 their rivalry spilled out in public. It was a usual morning at Gorakhpur railway station and the Shan-e-Awadh Express was ready to leave for Lucknow when shots rang out suddenly near the first-class compartment of the train. The sight was horrific as Ravindra Singh, a young MLA of the Janata Party, a Thakur, was found lying on the floor with blood gushing out of his chest. It soon became clear that he was shot by a group of men who had escaped in jeeps and motorcycles amid the hue and cry at the station. Singh, who was on his way to the state capital to attend the assembly session, was immediately rushed to the city hospital, where he died after three days. His murder shook the local politics of Gorakhpur, and the Thakurs suspected the shooting to be the handiwork of the Brahmins. It was at this point that Shahi launched himself as the leader of the Thakurs in the region and sounded the bugle of war against Harishankar Tiwari and his Brahmin gang.

Over the next two decades, both caste gangs clashed on innumerable occasions, and the Purvanchal region kept grabbing the headlines for its deadly gang wars. In 1985, Vir Bahadur Singh rose to the position of chief minister. His tenure proved to be a game-changer for the mafia dons of eastern UP as he launched a direct attack on their influence and hold in the region. He got Harishankar Tiwari and Virendra Pratap Shahi both arrested under the Uttar Pradesh Gangsters and Anti-Social Activities (Prevention) Act (commonly known as the Gangster Act). Eventually, this led the two criminals to seek full-time careers in active politics. But by then the Tiwari–Shahi rivalry had already changed the dynamics of UP politics.

From crime bosses, the two gangsters now became 'white-cloth' politicians. Tiwari even wore Gandhian attire. Both Tiwari and Shahi became MLAs by winning elections. This was just not possible without the well-organized and systematic backing of politicians of their own castes. And, since they operated under the patronage of their caste leaders, it was not possible for a long time for any new player to bypass this nexus.

This ushered in a new era in Uttar Pradesh where mafia members and dons entered politics and provided extraordinary stability to their criminal base. The success of Harishankar Tiwari was especially noteworthy. In 1985, he became the first person in the history of Indian politics to win an election (for the Congress) while in prison. Through his muscle power and influence in Gorakhpur, he went on to win from the Chillupar constituency of Gorakhpur district as many as six times. Shahi, too, twice became MLA from the Lakshmipur seat of Gorakhpur district, though he could not match the consistency of Tiwari's winning streak. Both Tiwari and Shahi fielded themselves as independents initially, but soon the biggest politicians from across party lines were seeking their patronage.

It is often seen in politics that instability makes way for political machinations and the entry of wrong players. In the case of Uttar Pradesh, this was what happened, and thereby the path was paved for a much larger role for these gangster-turned-politicians. The 1990s saw the rise of unstable coalition politics in UP, with no less than five chief ministers between 1996 and 2000. I myself witnessed the extreme instability of governments in UP as a reporter. Amidst their mergers and splits, the biggest challenge for political parties was to maintain their majority in the house, and this opened the floodgates for MPs and MLAs of a criminal background in UP politics.

But it was the Kalyan Singh government, formed in 1998, which most unabashedly accommodated politicians well known for their criminal backgrounds into the cabinet. One ministerial appointment that shook UP was that of Harishankar Tiwari as the science and technology minister. Tiwari was by no means a BJP or Kalyan Singh loyalist. Yet, he muscled his way into a UP government. Later, having contested on a Congress ticket, he also managed to get a cabinet rank appointment in the Mayawati and Mulayam Singh Yadav governments. This feat of Tiwari's illustrates the story of crime in UP politics in the 1990s.

Interestingly, it was in the late 1990s that Shri Prakash Shukla, a Brahmin and a 'new kid' from the Purvanchal region, started posing a challenge to the old-school mafia there. The entry of Shukla into the crime syndicate of UP created a sensation as he garnered the support of Suraj Bhan, a dreaded don from Bihar, and challenged the rules of the game almost single-handedly.

From the mid-1990s, Shukla, who had a swanky lifestyle and the ambition of becoming India's top gangster, started threatening the dominance of Virendra Pratap Shahi and Harishankar Tiwari in railway contracts. The ripple-effect of his rivalry with Shahi was especially felt in the region. It was believed that Shahi had a narrow escape in 1996 when Shukla, along with his mentor Suraj Bhan, attacked him in Gorakhpur. The very next year, Shukla became the most dreaded don of eastern UP almost overnight. In early 1997, he received information that Shahi was seeking a room to rent with his girlfriend in the Indira Nagar locality of Lucknow. For Shukla, it was a much-awaited opportunity as Shahi would not be with his men. He landed up there and fired at Shahi, emptying his magazine into him. Shahi died almost immediately. With his murder in the heart of Lucknow, Shukla made a big statement of his dominance in the underworld of UP.

In the following years, Shukla continued to terrorize UP and the state capital, which was then the constituency of Prime Minister Atal Bihari Vajpayee. On 26 May 1998, he again made a mockery of law and order in Lucknow. Around 7.30 a.m. that day, K.K. Rastogi, a businessman from an old and prominent Lucknow family, left his house along with his son Kunal for a drive to the Botanical Garden in the city. A white Maruti forced them to stop near Gokhale Marg; two armed men got out and dragged Kunal into their car, after which Rastogi tried to give them chase. This infuriated Shukla, who then shot Rastogi dead at close range. Such was the terror Shukla created among the business community of Lucknow that after the murder of K.K. Rastogi a process of issuing arms licences to the city's traders had to be expedited by the district magistrate of the time.[9]

It was also speculated that Harishankar Tiwari was on Shukla's hit list too, as Shukla had set his eyes on the Chillupar seat. But before Shukla could explore a career in politics, he was shot dead by a UP Special Task Force in Ghaziabad in 1998. The constitution of the STF was one of the stringent measures the Kalyan Singh government had to take in order to control the influence of gangsters in the region.

The deadly tussle that eastern UP witnessed between Shahi and Tiwari throughout the 1970s and '80s gave rise to many other criminals and, of course, to many rivalries between them. By the late 1990s, several of these men—including Raja Bhaiyya, Mukhtar Ansari, Munna Bajrangi, D.P. Yadav, Brijbhushan, Sharan Singh, Brajesh Singh and Amarmani Tripathi—had emerged as politicians too. In proportion to their muscle power and caste base, these criminals-turned-politicians controlled their own territories—Gorakhpur, Basti, Jaunpur, Allahabad, Rae Bareli, Pratapgarh—some even expanding their footprint beyond UP.[10] Their entry into the world of politics facilitated new alliances and networks they could now operate with. Their considerable sway in many different regions of UP was exploited by politicians for use against their arch rivals.

This period also witnessed the rise of don-turned-politician Mukhtar Ansari. By the late 1990s, Ansari had gained notoriety for his criminal activities in the districts of Mau, Ghazipur, Varanasi and Jaunpur. His tussle with Brajesh Singh, a Thakur from Varanasi who was another influential mafia-don of the region, was well known. Brajesh Singh was said to have killed sharp-shooter Haldhankar from Arun Gawli's gang, along with four policemen, in Mumbai's J.J. Hospital in a dispute over coal and liquor contracts. In 1996, Ansari succeeded in winning Mau constituency on a BSP ticket, and this sharpened his political clout decisively. He was now mentor to the most notorious criminals of eastern UP—Prem Prakash, alias Munna Bajrangi, and Sanjeev Maheshwari, alias Jiiva.[11] The Thakurs of the region were siding with Brajesh Singh under the leadership of BJP MLA Krishnanand Rai. The brutal and sensational murder of Rai in broad daylight in November 2005 was nothing but an outcome of the power play going on between Ansari and Singh.

While the gangster juggernaut kept rolling in the state, many parts of Purvanchal became shelters for ganglords, a very interesting and fascinating aspect of the crime syndicates that operated—and of the ones that now operate—in UP. The city of Mirzapur was most famous for this and was considered a safe haven for criminals during the heydays of Shahi, Tiwari and Ansari. In fact, it is still believed that Mirzapur was the operational base of Munna Bajrangi for most of the sensational murders he committed in the late 1990s. What made Mirzapur a shelter for criminals was its unique geographical location in UP: it touched many state borders, thus creating jurisdictional issues for police and administration; it was on the route of the Ganga; and, most importantly, it had the Chandraprabha Wildlife Sanctuary, where criminals could play hide-and-seek with the police.

Abu Salem, a familiar name in the Indian underworld, has links to UP and to Azamgarh, a small mofussil town in eastern UP which, till his notorious rise, was best known for the poet and writer Kaifi Azmi. Salem's story depicts how local UP dons extended their network to Mumbai and eventually to Dubai. Once a communist bastion, Azamgarh became so notorious that in the late 1990s it gained the distinction of being called the 'Dubai of UP'—and not in any complimentary way. This title was in recognition of its connections with the underworld of Mumbai and Dubai. Azamgarh also hit the headlines with the murder of music baron Gulshan Kumar in 1997.

Abu Salem's arrest in Portugal's capital city of Lisbon in 2005 was unexpected. There had been rumours—never confirmed till their official split—that Salem was beginning to have problems in Dawood's D-company with his aide Chhota Shakeel.[12] Salem was among the D-company's most dominant faces dealing with Mumbai and Bollywood. As a team of the Central Bureau of Investigation (CBI) rushed to Lisbon, so did a handful of journalists, I among them. Salem's arrest was a development that would forever alter equations in the D-company and its hold over both Bollywood and Mumbai. But what was also eagerly awaited was the layers of information expected to be unravelled with the arrest of Abu Salem. But, as I observed and later found out, Salem and his lawyers first made sure that it was impossible to prove that the man arrested was Abu Salem. For some time, he identified himself as a Pakistani, backed by a fake passport, and enjoyed a regular life with his actress-girlfriend Monica Bedi. I even visited the restaurant where the two were regulars, and when I spoke to the restaurant staff, they seemed to have no clue about Salem's real identity.

The Salem case was a long and hard-fought battle for the Indian government and the CBI to first prove in the Lisbon courts that the arrested person was indeed Abu Salem, not to mention the difficulty of getting him extradited to India. In the process, Salem ensured that there would be no death penalty for him because the country in which he was arrested did not have capital punishment.

Salem's Azamgarh connection was revealed for the first time during the investigations into Gulshan Kumar's murder, when police recovered a cache of arms from the shooters, which had 'Made in Bamhaur' inscribed on them. The police agencies later located Bamhaur in Azamgarh district. It was a small village near Mir Sarai, Salem's native place. By that time Salem had risen well in his 'calling', already managing the affairs of the Dawood Ibrahim gang.

It was believed that Salem came in contact with the underworld of Mumbai in 1985, when he was assigned the task of transporting the D-gang's arms and ammunition from one part of the city to another. Those were the days when Salem ran electronics shop in the Andheri locality of Mumbai. He soon became an influential member of the gang and started extorting money from builders, Bollywood directors and producers. Through his underworld connections and influence he was able to flee the country with Bedi before being extradited to India in 2005.

Throughout his stay in Mumbai, and later in Dubai in the 1990s, Salem was always in touch with the local crime syndicates operating in eastern UP. One of the key reasons for the success of both Abu Salem and the local mafia-dons of UP was the consistent supply line of shooters that Azamgarh and nearby places provided. As I reported closely on the Mumbai police when based in the city in 2003, the top cops made me understand how it worked.

In the business of contract killing, although the price of a contract, or *supari*, was very high, the young men who executed it were paid very little, in fact peanuts. They were bought to Mumbai to execute the crime from places like Azamgarh, the biggest advantage in employing them being that they had no prior criminal history as far as Mumbai Police was concerned. Despite knowing these young men's bosses, Mumbai Police was almost crippled when it came to finding the shooters if they were not caught on the spot. These young men, after executing the crime assigned to them, rapidly disappeared from Mumbai, eventually reaching Nepal because of the porous borders between that country and eastern UP. Some even made it to Dubai. This arrangement went on very effectively in the 1990s, while back home in UP the mafia bosses were turning politicians. To date, Abu Salem is regarded as the key link between UP's crime lords and the Mumbai underworld. As I could see, and as has been reported by journalists over the years, it was through these means that many gangsters, after fleeing the country successfully, managed to operate from outside India.

It was believed that Salem kept an eye on the criminal activities of the region by means of the phone booths that mushroomed in the locality during late 1990s, which eventually became well-known as channels for communication between UP and the Gulf region. Incidentally, Azamgarh and Mau also gained notoriety for being centres of *hawala* transactions during the same period. Local *hawala* operators also used the same phone booths the underworld did to access the Mumbai and Dubai dons. I can recall how in the late 1990s, the infusion of *hawala* money into the local economy of Azamgarh spectacularly transformed the landscape of the city. One could easily spot luxury marble houses in the interiors of the city, and this surprised many first-time visitors.

The city of Azamgarh also made headlines for the caste rivalry between its Yadavs and Thakurs. The architect of this rivalry in Azamgarh was Ramakant Yadav, a mafia-member-turned-politician who entered the crime syndicate of eastern UP in the 1990s. Yadav came into the limelight for the first time in 1988 when he buried alive a Thakur family. And then, like every Bahubali in the region, he was patronized by all the major political parties. He started with the Congress, then shifted his loyalty to SP, then to the BSP, finally ending up as an MP on a BJP ticket in 2009. Umakant Yadav, a cousin of Ramakant's, was another player who helped extend the hegemony of the Yadavs in the region.

The rivalry between Mukhtar Ansari and Brajesh Singh frequently sent tremors through the region. There were other rivalries too during this time. The Ramayan-Sadhu gang challenged the supremacy of Ramakant Yadav in Azamgarh.

Their clashing claims over liquor contracts led to several conflicts between these two gangs in the 2000s. It was believed that the Ramayan-Sadhu gang had an edge in these clashes as it managed to acquire several AK-47 rifles.

The very surreal stories of caste and crime in UP would be incomplete without the telling of the Bandit Queen story. It's important to understand how the teenaged Phoolan Devi turned into a dacoit. Born into a very poor, lower-caste Nishad or Mallah family in Jalaun district of Uttar Pradesh, Phoolan Devi had a troubled childhood, often finding herself in situations where she and her parents had to do the bidding of the higher-caste Thakurs in their village. An early incident from her life reflects the great sense of pride Phoolan had even at that young age. Her family was cheated of their inheritance—a portion of land—by Phoolan's own uncle, and young Phoolan fought a high-spirited battle to reclaim her family's right from the uncle. During this dispute he repeatedly insulted and abused her. Phoolan Devi's temper also did not go down well with those who called the shots in the region, and the poor Nishad family was warned and threatened by the dominant Thakurs of the region that Phoolan was a threat to the village system. It was under these circumstances that the eleven-year-old Phoolan was married off to a man three times her age, bringing her childhood days to an abrupt end.

But her ordeals were far from over. She made several attempts to run away; she later said she was fleeing her own husband, who had repeatedly abused her sexually. Even when Phoolan

Devi somehow managed to return to her parents' home, she was accused by a cousin of burgling her home, as a result of which Phoolan Devi ended up being imprisoned for a whole month. There, she claimed, she was physically tortured. The year was 1979, and she was just sixteen years old.

Having spent time in prison and having been sexually abused many times, it was highly unlikely that Phoolan Devi and her family could survive peacefully in their Thakur-dominated village. The only option left to the family was to get Phoolan Devi to return to her husband's home, but she again ran away from there to avoid sexual exploitation. Left with nowhere to go, Phoolan Devi was forced to look for shelter in the dreaded Chambal ravines, and this proved to be the biggest turning point of her life, eventually leading to her becoming the 'Bandit Queen' of the region.

The main gang operating in the region was led by Babu Gujjar, a dominant upper-caste man. Since Phoolan Devi was the only woman to enter in the gang world of Chambal, it was predictable that the gang leader would eye her, eventually making her his moll. But Phoolan Devi was not ready to accept the supremacy of Babu Gujjar. His attempts to convince Phoolan Devi to submit to him repeatedly failed; Babu Gujjar now decided that he would subdue her through physical assault. It was at this time that another gang member, Vikram Mallah, belonging to the same caste as Phoolan, came into the scene. He murdered Babu Gujjar, declared himself the leader of the gang and took Phoolan Devi as his lover, thereby protecting her from others. One of the important implications of the coming together of Phoolan Devi and Vikram Mallah was that the gang rivalries of the Chambal region took on a clear caste orientation, with the dominant Thakurs on one side and the Nishads on the other.

For the next couple of years, both Phoolan Devi and Vikram Mallah carried out several attacks in the region, the most famous of them being the one on Phoolan Devi's own husband's village. It was carried out in broad daylight, and Phoolan Devi herself dragged her husband out of his house and stabbed him in front of the villagers, leaving them numb and terrorized. Though her husband did not die, her gang left him lying on the road in a pool of blood, with a warning note that older men should not marry young girls. This was just the beginning of Phoolan Devi's reputation as a terror in the heartland of the Chambal region. The dramatic style of Phoolan Devi and her gang members also gained notoriety; they often disguised themselves as policemen and looted trucks and containers on the highways. Landowners, often upper-caste Thakurs, also became targets of the gang. This was hardly surprising, considering Phoolan Devi's old caste rivalry with the Thakurs.

The decisive challenge to Phoolan Devi and Vikram Mallah came from two Thakur dacoits, Sri Ram Singh and Lala Ram Singh, who were in jail at the time of Babu Gujjar's murder and who had successfully managed to escape from prison before finally joining the gang led by the two Nishads, Vikram Mallah and Phoolan Devi, only to betray them later. In a rather direct challenge to Vikram Mallah's authority in the gang, Sri Ram Singh and Lala Ram Singh killed him while he was sleeping and abducted Phoolan Devi. She was taken to the village of Behmai, less than 100 kilometres from Kanpur, where she was reportedly tortured, assaulted and gang-raped by Thakur men for a period of three whole weeks. Phoolan Devi had never before been subjected to such intense violence and torture. In fact, her torture might have gone on but for some of her gang members, who had once been loyal to her lover Vikram Mallah, coming to her rescue.

After managing to escape from Sri Ram Singh and Lala Ram Singh, Phoolan Devi mobilized Vikram Mallah's loyalists. A key name in this gang was Man Singh Mallah, a Nishad whom Phoolan Devi trusted most after Vikram Mallah's death. This clearly meant a new wave of Thakur and Nishad rivalry in Chambal, and it was easy to speculate that both would, sooner or later, clash in the region. However, for almost seventeen months Phoolan Devi and her gang members did not have any clue as to where Sri Ram Singh and Lala Ram Singh might be hiding. Finally, on 14 February 1981, Phoolan Devi and her gang members stormed into the same Behmai village where she had been captured. At the time of their strike, the Thakurs were preparing for a wedding. The attack was well planned. Phoolan Devi split her forces into three to cover the entire village. She herself led the force that took the direct path to the village. At the wedding venue, she first of all demanded to have Sri Ram Singh and Lala Ram Singh brought out, but they were not to be found. Nobody would even give her a hint as to where the two Thakurs were. Incensed at the silence, Phoolan Devi ordered her gang members to line up every Thakur man at the venue. They were lined up and shot by her gang members at her command. Twenty-two of them died on the spot.

It was an operation typical of Phoolan Devi's attacks, except that here the motive was purely revenge. This attack came to be known as the 'Behmai massacre'. Almost every media report highlighted Phoolan Devi's role as the undisputed daredevil dacoit queen of the region who had successfully avenged her sexual assault. The incident naturally shook the political circles in the state. It was not only an incident that pointed to the complete failure of law and order in the state but also demonstrated that the deadliest face of crime pivoted on caste in the state. The political fallout of the incident was therefore inevitable. UP chief minister V.P. Singh immediately resigned, taking moral responsibility for the massacre. This was perhaps the first instance in the history of UP politics when caste rivalry resulting in a bloodbath ultimately led a chief minister to resign.

Though the Behmai massacre made Phoolan Devi a legendary figure in the crime world of UP and Madhya Pradesh, which was clearly the climactic point of her criminal career, her influence declined considerably in a span of just two years. This was largely due to her deteriorating health and the massive crackdown by police forces in the interiors of Chambal. Many of Phoolan Devi's gang members had died in these two years. This was now the right time for Phoolan Devi to seek political patronage, so she planned a backdoor surrender to the authorities in 1983, of course, on terms and conditions set by her.

As part of these terms, she agreed to surrender to the Arjun Singh-led Congress government of Madhya Pradesh, having secured a promise that she would be spared the death penalty. One of the conditions of the surrender was that she would lay down her arms before the pictures of Mahatma Gandhi and goddess Durga. The day of her surrender in Bhind in Madhya Pradesh turned out to be a curious and momentous event witnessed by an audience of almost 10,000, including Arjun Singh. The Bandit

Queen of Chambal was charged with as many as forty-eight crimes, including thirty charges of banditry and kidnapping. Her trials in all these matters dragged on for over eleven years, which she spent as an undertrial in the Gwalior and Jabalpur jails.[13]

Phoolan Devi's fortunes changed dramatically in 1994. The 1990s were the heyday of Mandal-Kamandal politics in Uttar Pradesh and the Centre. With the rise of the Yadavs under the leadership of Mulayam Singh Yadav and Dalits under the leadership of Mayawati, different caste combinations played out in UP, making and unmaking several governments during this period. One of the interesting and far-reaching implications of the churn in the backward-caste politics of the 1990s was the direct entry of mafia members and gangsters, often allied to rival caste groups, in the active politics of UP. They brought considerable muscle power and influence to the parties they joined and held a tight control on the caste groups they belonged to. It was at the peak of this backward-caste politics that the ground for Phoolan Devi's entry into UP politics was prepared by then chief minister Mulayam Singh Yadav.

As a first move, Phoolan Devi was released on parole in 1994 on the intervention of Vishambhar Prasad Nishad, the leader of the Mallah caste of boatmen to which Phoolan belonged. But Mulayam Singh Yadav went a step further; his government withdrew all charges against her in 1994 and cleared her way to enter politics. After two years of her release from jail, she contested the 1996 Lok Sabha election as a member of Mulayam Singh Yadav's Samajwadi Party from the Nishad-dominated Mirzapur constituency and registered a thumping victory. She served for two years, from 1996 to 1998, as a parliamentarian from Mirzapur and was re-elected from the same seat in the 1999 general election. But she was gunned down midway into her term by a Thakur, Sher Singh Rana, on 25 July 2001 outside her Delhi bungalow.

As we look at the caste angle to organized crime in UP, the story of the most elusive bandit leader of Chambal, Shiv Kumar Patel, or Dadua, too warrants attention. Like Phoolan Devi, Dadua also operated in the ravines and forests on the border between Uttar Pradesh and Madhya Pradesh for almost three decades. He was a Kurmi, a backward[14] caste of UP's Gangetic plains, and came from Devkali village near Chitrakoot.

Dadua made a sensational entry on the crime scene of the region in the late 1970s by killing eight upper-caste people, mostly Brahmins, who had allegedly paraded his father nude in his village over a conflict and then brutally murdered him in broad daylight. Dadua had been twenty-two at that time. Immediately after he had avenged his father's murder, he fled to the forests of Patha in the Chambal–Yamuna valley, never to return to his native village as Shiv Kumar Patel.

Dadua entered the crime world of Bundelkhand at a point when several dacoit gangs were already operating in the region. The first task before him was to accommodate himself in one of the gangs, a common strategic requirement for any new player entering the world of dacoity. The safest move for new players was to align themselves with gang leaders from their own caste. Here, another Kurmi and dreaded dacoit of the region, Gaya Kurmi, baptized Dadua. Having worked closely with the Raja

Rangoli gang, another notorious group active in the valley, Gaya Kurmi knew the nitty-gritty of the dacoit business. Interestingly, it was Gaya Kurmi who had equipped the Kurmi gang with modern carbines, sten-guns and magnum rifles in the late 1970s and early 1980s when other gangs were mostly relying on country-made weapons.

From Gaya Kurmi, Dadua soon learnt enough tricks to run a dacoit business of its own. But by then the Uttar Pradesh government, under the leadership of Vir Bahadur Singh—who was a Thakur and hailed from the same place as Gaya Kurmi—had embarked on a massive crackdown on dacoits operating in the Bundelkhand region. Naturally, Gaya Kurmi was on the hit-list of the police. Realizing that he may not be able to save himself from being killed by the police, Gaya Kurmi chalked out a plan. He reportedly handed over his arsenal of automated rifles and guns to Dadua while he himself surrendered to the police near Majhganva village in Banda, Uttar Pradesh.

According to the plan, Dadua was to threaten anyone standing against Gaya Kurmi as witness, and that's exactly what Dadua did as Gaya Kurmi's loyalist whenever witnesses stood up to testify against his mentor. Finally, after just four years, Gaya Kurmi was freed from all the charges levelled against him, in the absence of witnesses. In the meantime, Dadua had established himself as the lord of the Kurmi gang.

With sophisticated guns and rifles in his armoury, Dadua's reign of terror in the Banda–Chitrakoot region of Uttar Pradesh intensified in the 1980s. As his influence rose, he virtually controlled the entire economy of Bundelkhand. It is believed that he received a cut from all contracts in the area, ranging from construction and irrigation to telecom deals.[15] He notoriously earned a huge amount of money from the tendu leaf trade. Tendu had the same significance for the brigand that sandalwood had for Veerappan, the bandit who operated in Karnataka, Kerala and Tamil Nadu. This was also one of the reasons why he used to be known as the Veerappan of Bundelkhand.

Dadua and his Kurmi gang only gained in notoriety as the years passed. They now had a new modus operandi of conducting sensational kidnappings and murders—and their victims were often well-heeled Brahmins of the region. In 1984, Dadua abducted three relatives of the block-pramukh of Karvi, Hira Pandey, a Brahmin, and later shot them dead. He went on to kidnap a fifteen-year-old Brahmin boy near Kanpur Dehat while he was on his way back home from school. Mostly his victims succumbed to his demands without even informing the police—such was the terror of Dadua among the Brahmins of the Mau and Banda regions.

One of the most shocking crimes he committed was the murder of a high court judge and a couple of his relatives in 1982 near Banda. It later turned out that the judge was the elder brother of the UP chief minister of the time, V.P. Singh. Such daredevilry on the part of Dadua's gang kept the police forces of the state on their toes for almost three decades, when every new crime by the Dadua gang surpassed its preceding one in scale of violence and brutality.

On 23 July 1986, Dadua orchestrated one of his gang's biggest massacres ever in Ramu ka Purva village near Banda. Infuriated at the arrest of a close relative of a kingpin of his gang, Dadua and his men entered the village around 6 p.m. and slayed nine villagers. They were picked from five different families, tied to a pole and riddled with bullets. Some other villagers, including some women, were dragged out of their homes, humiliated and tortured, leaving everyone paralysed in fear. Media reports mentioned how terror-stricken women themselves gave Dadua the keys to boxes containing their jewellery and valuables, which he eventually looted. So traumatized were the survivors at the spot that they could barely muster the courage to talk about what had happened that dreadful evening.

The Kurmi gang targeted and dealt with police informers in a similar heinous manner. Every time they attacked a village, they would threaten the villagers against tipping off the police about their activities and operations. If they did sound out the police, Dadua would get them shot.

Throughout his reign of terror, one question remained largely unanswered: how did Dadua and his Kurmi gang manage to elude police forces so consistently in the Bundelkhand region? Why did attempts by successive governments to chase and hunt down the Kurmi gang always fail? The answer to these questions lies in one of the most ironic but revealing aspects of UP politics. For sure, the tactics Dadua had learnt over the years as a dacoit had played a role in this: he was always on the move and never rested more than a few hours at a place. Rarely did he or his men leave any trace behind them after their operations.

But the real reason for his successful elusiveness was the political backing he was able to garner from time to time in Uttar Pradesh. The fact that he belonged to the Kurmi caste, which formed almost 40 per cent of the population of Banda, Chitrakoot and nearby areas, made him a serious contender for the Brahmins who comprised 35 per cent of the total population in these areas. He was thus increasingly backed by backward-caste leaders to counter the influence Brahmins had in the region. It was this political backing that made a mockery of the ambitious Operation Dadua launched by Vir Bahadur Singh to bring him to heel.

Under this mission, which cost the UP government over Rs 3 crore, the Provincial Armed Constabulary (PAC) was deployed in the 120 sq km area of Bundelkhand, but it did not succeed in engaging the gang even in a single encounter. The reason, of course, was the suspected links many forest department officials and politicians had with Dadua and his Kurmi gang. In fact, this was repeatedly cited by Vir Bahadur Singh as one of the reasons that derailed Operation Dadua.

Despite his considerable influence and political backing in the Kurmi-dominated pockets of the Bundelkhand region, Dadua confined himself merely to playing the role of persuader, often changing sides and influencing voters as per the orders of his political godfathers. With the political backing of Ramsajeevan Singh, a BSP parliamentarian from Banda, Dadua is believed to have manipulated the voting in ten Lok Sabha seats in the Chambal region in the 1989 general election.

But from the late 1990s, the traditional relationship between the Chambal dacoits and their political godfathers started to change significantly. Recognizing the role of dacoits in the power game, almost every political party was fielding them as candidates. It was at this point that Dadua smelt an opportunity in politics and planned for his possible surrender. There were rumours that he was eyeing the Banda seat, but his plan to surrender did not materialize, owing to some conflicts in the terms he proposed for it.

In the 2000s, he dramatically changed his affiliation from the BSP to SP. SP leader Shayamcharan Gupta paved the way for not only Dadua's but his entire family's entry into Mulayam Singh Yadav's party. This, naturally, infuriated Ramsajeevan Singh, who was Dadua's old political mentor in the BSP as well as Shayamcharan Gupta's arch rival. With the defeat of Ramsajeevan Singh from the Banda seat in the 2004 Lok Sabha election, Dadua's relations with the BSP further deteriorated, which ultimately resulted in his encounter killing by the UP Special Task Force in 2007.

The story of the crafty and colourful Nirbhay Singh Gujjar is also unique in many respects in UP's modern history of organized crime based on caste. Born into a lower-caste Gujjar family near the Etawah district of Uttar Pradesh, Nirbhay Singh Gujjar is often hailed as the last lion of the Chambal.

He rose to power in the region in the late-1990s, when the romanticized image of the Chambal dacoit was going through a phase of transition. While the old dacoits of the region were desperately seeking full-time careers in active politics, new *baaghis* were finding their place in pockets of Bundelkhand. These new entrants used modern methods of communication. In the 1990s, criminal gangs had stopped raiding villages and were instead relying on extortion, protection rackets and violence during the time of elections. This was the tactical flexibility required on their part to adjust to the changes that were happening during those years.

One such change was the expansion of the limits of towns in the central parts of UP, which made it increasingly difficult for dacoits to attack villages nearby. Their motivations to enter the crime world of the Chambal were more or less the same as earlier, however. Many wanted to dethrone the raj of rival caste groups in particular regions and in return got the patronage of their political lords. So, while the spirit and technique of their operations changed significantly, the caste angle to the dacoit culture of Chambal remained intact. The rise of Nirbhay Singh Gujjar marked all these changes to a lesser or a greater degree.

Though the first official case against Nirbhay Gujjar was registered in 1989, he gained notoriety only in the 1990s when he started to execute kidnappings for ransom or extort money on a huge scale, creating a reign of terror in the districts of eastern and central UP. He was known to have mobilized more than seventy dacoits for his gang in a very short period of time—which was evidence of his rising dominance in large parts of Uttar Pradesh and Madhya Pradesh. But the biggest reason why Nirbhay Singh Gujjar became a consummate folk anti-hero in the vast Chambal region during his peak in the mid-1990s and early-2000s was his modern, lavish lifestyle as well as the techniques he introduced to the dacoit gangs of the Chambal.

He was the first dacoit in the region to reportedly use cell phones and sim cards for his operations, not to forget his arsenal of AK-47 rifles, shotguns, bulletproof jackets and night-vision binoculars that facilitated his movement in the region. His sharp communication network of cell phones changed the conventional rules of the dacoity business almost immediately for him. He could now talk to his political lords sitting in Lucknow with greater ease. Keeping an eye on the activities of his own gang members and those of rival gang members also became easier for him. In fact, this allowed him to start an altogether new culture in the region—the satellite gang culture—where he himself did not undertake any operations but sent various gangs to execute kidnappings and extortions on behalf of him in return for a small portion of the loot. This was purely a business deal, where a big player was outsourcing work to smaller players for a small payment.

In another sharp departure from the older dacoity culture, Nirbhay Singh Gujjar invited the media and gave interviews on a number of occasions. While earlier dreaded bandits like Phoolan Devi and Dadua played hide-and-seek with police agencies and made sure they were rarely seen in public, Nirbhay Singh Gujjar loved media visibility (but he also made sure his exact location was never revealed in public).

Throughout his time at the top of his game, Nirbhay Singh Gujjar lived lavishly—another interesting aspect of his life. He was a womanizer, often abducting women forcefully and making them stay with him as his lovers. However, despite having married thrice—in the jungles—to women he had abducted, all his wives ran away with other men. His last wife Neelam, whom he kidnapped when she was just twenty, hit the headlines when she eloped with one of his gang members. The man she ran away with was Nirbhay Singh Gujjar's own foster son Shyam Jatav, who betrayed Gujjar in 2004. Jatav himself was the son of an influential Delhi businessman, Dalchandra Jatav, and was notoriously kidnapped by Nirbhay Singh Gujjar in the 1990s when he was just nine years old. Over the years, Shyam Jatav was reportedly trained by Gujjar to take over the control of the gang. It was also widely reported later that Nirbhay Singh Gujjar declared a reward of Rs 21 lakh to anyone who could bring him Neelam and Shyam Jatav, dead or alive.

This declaration was made by Gujjar at a dacoit panchayat, another new mechanism of his creation, which became notorious in the early 2000s. This panchayat was created as a collective response by the dacoit gangs of the Chambal valley, and was led by Nirbhay Gujjar, Pahalwan Singh Gurjar, Ram Asre, alias Phakkad, and Man Singh. The objective was to teach the police of Uttar Pradesh and Madhya Pradesh a lesson for their attempts to curtail the gangs' dominance in the region, which had been happening from 2000 onwards. It was through these panchayats that Nirbhay Singh Gujjar influenced the local politics of the region, issuing orders from these platforms and punishing whoever defied them. During the 2004 gram pradhan election in Kurcha village near Akbarpur in the state, he allegedly cut off the nose of the gram pradhan, a Thakur.

Nirbhay Singh Gujjar fielded his own candidates several times in local elections as no other candidate would contest, fearing him. Soon, Nirbhay Singh Gujjar openly started campaigning for the Samajwadi Party of the Yadavs, ensuring his support to Mulayam Singh Yadav's party in successive elections. However, by the time Mulayam Singh Yadav became the chief minister of the state in 2003, Nirbhay Singh Gujjar's influence in the Chambal region was on the decline. There were rumours that the desertion by his wife Neelam had made him emotionally weak and that he was no longer in a position to lead the gang.

It was ironic that the same new dacoity culture that Nirbhay Singh Gujjar had started in the Chambal region brought a dramatic end to his own life. His new culture of interacting with the media proved to be the costliest mistake of his life. In July 2005, during a media interaction, he openly disclosed his relations with the Samajwadi Party and even went on to say that he was negotiating his surrender with Mulayam Singh Yadav, who would be offering him a Lok Sabha ticket in the next general election in return. This open admission of his linkages with the Samajwadi Party infuriated Mulayam Singh Yadav, who then ordered his administration to hunt down and finish the Gujjar gang of the Chambal. The Uttar Pradesh Special Task Force got into action, chased Nirbhay Singh Gujjar for almost three months and finally gunned him down in November 2005 in Chief Minister Mulayam Singh Yadav's home district of Etawah. At the time of his death, Gujjar had 203 criminal cases lodged against him, including thirty-two for murder and 150 for kidnapping for ransom.

Thus, from the Bandit Queen Phoolan Devi to Dadua, and then to Nirbhay Singh Gujjar and many others, the Chambal valley of Uttar Pradesh kept producing dacoits and criminals of extraordinary influence who shook the politics of the state from time to time. While all these dacoits represented different caste groups and employed different modus operandi to extend their dominance in the region, the way they were dealt with by their political lords shared a remarkable similarity: they were politically backed to counter a rival caste group, were brought into politics as major players when it suited politicians to do so, and of course were ousted and got rid of when they no longer served any purpose.

While links between crime and politics obtained in many states and their nexus was a big subject of national debate, the caste base and caste conflicts behind organized crime in UP make the stories of the crime world from this state unique. For the same reason, it was easy for the leaders of criminal gangs to make their way into politics in UP as they were not held back by any loyalty towards a particular political leader or party. In that lay their success.

6

The Polarization Plank

In this book, where I have tried to deep-dive into a dark and (so far) unchangeable reality of Indian and UP politics since Independence, which is caste, it is also equally important to discuss another reality—polarization, and the various ways in which all political parties have used it to appeal to their core base from time to time. This tactic has been used by all political parties since the early 1990s and up to the present day. UP politics was obviously plagued by caste equations that played a dominant role in the selection of candidates for elections. It was also clear that as and when the need arose to consolidate their vote base, leaders in UP never shied away from appeasing it in one way or another.

It was on a cold winter's night of 1977 that a middle-aged man knocked on the door of a house in the Dalit basti of Inderpuri in west Delhi. As the door was opened, the man introduced himself as Kanshi Ram, president of the Backward and Minority Communities Employees Federation (BAMCEF). He wanted to invite Mayawati, who at that time was a young Indian Administrative Service (IAS) aspirant, to deliver a speech on the occasion of Ambedkar's birth anniversary. Those were the days when Kanshi Ram was trying to bring together educated Dalits from all over the country under his umbrella organization. He went on to ask Mayawati why she was preparing for the civil services exam. She replied that she wanted to serve the people of her community, to which Kanshi Ram famously replied that he would make Mayawati a leader whom many IAS officers would line up to serve. She would then be able to serve the interests of *apne log*—Dalits—with more authority and power.

In many ways, it was this politics of *apne log*—people of one's own community—that became dominant in Uttar Pradesh in the late 1990s, decisively changing the rules of politics in the state. Kanshi Ram and Mayawati were not alone in pushing themselves as guardians of their community. It was in the same period that Mulayam Singh Yadav launched himself as the leader of the Yadavs. Then there was the BJP, a party rapidly emerging in Hindi-speaking states as the protector of the Hindus. And above all, there was the Congress, the grand old party, witnessing its own downfall in UP and alternately employing, according to its critics, strategies of Hindu and Muslim appeasement amidst this rise of the Samajwadi Party (which chiefly appealed to the Yadavs and Muslims), the Bahujan Samaj Party (to Dalits) and the Bharatiya Janata Party (to caste Hindus). The polarization of electorates along the lines of Dalit, Hindu, Muslim and Yadav was extraordinary.

The politics of polarization was clearly linked with the slump of the Congress in Uttar Pradesh. Though the party, riding the sympathy wave following Indira Gandhi's assassination, had routed all opposition in the 1984 general election, it continued to lose its support base across all sections of society in the succeeding years. To make good this loss, Prime Minister

Rajiv Gandhi, advised by his key strategists, decided to play the polarization card. For one, as mentioned earlier, he had the gates of the Ram Janmabhoomi opened. And before that, there had been the Shah Bano case, which created a lot of anxiety among Muslim hardliners, who saw the 1985 judgement of the Supreme Court as a threat to the decades-old Muslim personal laws. The apex court had ruled that a divorced Muslim woman was entitled to claim an allowance and maintenance from her ex-husband.

This had infuriated many Muslim clerics and some ministers in Rajiv's own cabinet. One of them was Ziaur Rahman Ansari. It was somewhere around 1985 that Ansari went to Gandhi and offered his resignation during the uproar over the court's verdict. Gandhi tore up his resignation letter and asked him to speak on the issue in Parliament. Ansari went on to deliver a fiery speech in the house, calling the court's verdict discriminatory and full of contradictions. It was believed that his speech was the first sign of Rajiv Gandhi's position on the issue. The prime minister finally brought in a law overturning the court's judgement in 1986 in the face of mounting pressure from Muslim ulemas. The overturning of this judgement by the Rajiv Gandhi government in many ways prepared the ground for the politics of polarization, the results of which were soon to become clear.

There was an inevitable Hindu backlash over the move by the Rajiv Gandhi government. Rajiv Gandhi's action was regarded by the VHP and other affiliates of the RSS as a step to appease the Muslims of the country. These parties were by then demanding more fiercely the construction of a Ram temple at Ayodhya.

In 1987, Swedish Radio claimed that Swedish arms manufacturer Bofors had paid bribes amounting to nearly

Rs 1,500 crore to top Indian politicians and defence personnel for the supply of arms to India by the company. This revelation shook national politics and the Rajiv Gandhi government. The fact that Rajiv Gandhi himself was implicated in the case hit hard his image of 'Mister Clean'. Realizing that the Congress was on the back foot politically, the VHP called its third Dharam Sansad in February 1989 in Allahabad and announced the date for the inauguration of the proposed Ram temple—9 November 1989. This announcement by the VHP was huge, and it changed the dynamics of UP politics forever. It was after this VHP Dharam Sansad that the BJP, for the first time, supported the Ram Janmabhoomi movement officially, adopting it as part of its political plank. The decision was taken at the party's historic 1989 Palampur session in Himachal Pradesh.

The situation was tricky for the Congress, though, as it had never been aloof from Ram Janmabhoomi affairs. It was believed that the Faizabad district court's order of opening the gates of the controversial Ram Janmabhoomi complex on 1 February 1986 had come directly from New Delhi, from the Prime Minister's Office itself.[16] Recalling this day, journalist Hemant Sharma says: 'I was present on that day in Ayodhya, and for me this was one of those rare moments in the history of independent India when the order of a court was followed within forty minutes of its declaration. The court gave its verdict at 4.40 p.m. and the locks of the complex were opened at 5.20 p.m. Clearly, the script for this eventful day was written in the national capital and Faizabad's local administration was aware of Delhi's directive.'

Many political observers of the time saw this court verdict as part of the party's larger strategy to win the Hindu vote, which it was quickly losing after its reversal of the Supreme Court judgement in the Shah Bano case. But then, with the VHP finalizing and announcing the date for the inauguration of a Ram temple in Ayodhya, the momentum shifted in favour of the BJP. The fact that the BJP came out in support of the Ram Janmabhoomi issue politically further forced the Congress to rethink its Ayodhya strategy.

Prime Minister Rajiv Gandhi called a meeting of his loyalists and key strategists on 16 October 1989, hoping to find a way out of the situation for the Congress. In an unexpected and dramatic move, Rajiv Gandhi decided to dissolve the Lok Sabha. Soon, dates for the next general election were announced—22 and 26 November, almost two weeks after the scheduled *shilanyaas* ceremony at Ayodhya. These dates were revealing—Rajiv Gandhi was preparing to capitalize on the Ram Janmabhoomi issue. He launched his electoral campaign from Ayodhya and repeatedly mentioned in his public rallies that his party was committed to bring 'Ram Rajya' to the country. But the outcome of the election came as a rude shock to the party and to Rajiv. His strategy of appeasing both Hindus and Muslims misfired, and he spectacularly failed to deliver at the ballot box. In Uttar Pradesh itself, the Congress was reduced to just fifteen seats.

The reversal of the court verdict in the Shah Bano case and the opening of the locks of the Ram Janmabhoomi structure made it evident that the Congress was very confused and had handled neither issue well. After 1989, the Congress lost most of the space it had occupied in UP, slumping to new lows in the state election after election. This confusion on the part of the Congress opened the floodgates for a more brazen version of polarization spearheaded by the BJP in a much more formidable and more impactful way than could have ever been imagined. The impact of this on national politics was deep and led to the emergence of big new players in the 'secular' space to take on the BJP in this polarized environment.

When Ayodhya was sweeping the headlines in national politics, something interesting was going on in other parts of the state, something that went unnoticed until 1989, when Mulayam Singh Yadav, a rustic man from the village of Saifai in Uttar Pradesh, rose to power and became the chief minister.

Mulayam, who was famously known as Chhote Lohia in political circles, who eventually was also called 'secular Mulayam', had served as the state's cooperative minister in the coalition government of UP formed after the Emergency. From the early 1980s, he began to tweak his socialist background to his own convenience, and the slump of the Congress in the 1989 election provided him the opportunity for which he had waited long. He joined hands with the Janata Dal spearheaded by V.P. Singh, a party that was by then a conglomerate of socialists and disgruntled Congressmen. Both the leftist and rightist forces were supporting it. It was time for Mulayam Singh Yadav to push his cards for the state's top post. A clever man, he successfully sidelined his main rival, Ajit Singh, and rose to the position of chief minister, leaving political observers surprised.

The brief tenure of Mulayam Singh Yadav proved to be very crucial for the politics of Uttar Pradesh as it was in these years that another script in the politics of polarization in the state was cleverly written. An important face of this politics was Mulayam Singh Yadav himself. It was clear that in the name of socialism and secularism, he was in fact helping the cause of his own caste—the Yadavs. The fallout of the Mandal agitation further helped him project himself as a leader representing the backward segments of Uttar Pradesh. His bold decision to order firing on the kar sevaks at the height of the Ram temple movement also made him appear as the saviour of Muslims.

For years it was this Yadav–Muslim combination that worked wonders for him in polarized UP.

7
The Bastions

For all these long years that I have looked at UP as a journalist, one of the most distinctive features of its politics is the string of political heavyweights that emerged from the state to become prime ministers, chief ministers and king-makers in Indian politics. It was natural that these leaders had their political pocket-boroughs, which I call their 'bastions'. But despite UP having produced politicians of national significance, the region itself could never transform for the better. And this is the story of UP—the state from where the biggest names in Indian politics have emerged but which continues to remain unreasonably backward.

My trip to my birthplace of Varanasi in 2014 was a most unusual one. Never before in the past had the city seen the kind of political buzz it did when Narendra Modi declared that he would contest the 2014 Lok Sabha elections from here. On 23 April 2014, Varanasi, the preeminent holy city of Hindus, was under the spotlight of national and international television media. The temple city was crawling with cameras and television crews, and the local people were finding it difficult to adjust to the atmospherics that filled the city. The sheer number of OB vans in the streets of the city left them overwhelmed. Varanasi, as a city of shrines and palaces, had always been of religious significance to them and they had seen it draw people from across the country in the millions. But at no point in the past had the city drawn so much attention for political reasons. The most promising face of the elections was being fielded from their city. As the locals watched the BJP's prime ministerial candidate Modi filing his nomination papers from the city, it was clear that Varanasi was going to be the talking point of the entire nation during the 2014 general election.

While the locals of Varanasi were perplexed at the extraordinary publicity a city of supposedly religious significance was getting in national politics, for many long-time observers of Uttar Pradesh politics, including me, this was not at all surprising. Having travelled extensively across Maharashtra and Gujarat and having constantly heard about 'Modi's Banaras', to me the party's decision to field its prime ministerial candidate from one of the key cities of the Purvanchal region of Uttar Pradesh was a familiar strategy and formula many political parties had already used in past: to choose Uttar Pradesh and especially the Purvanchal region of the state as their electoral battlefield; to set the tone for the election from there and amplify it rhetorically to maximize their electoral gains across the country.

In fact, I started my election coverage of UP from another place of enormous political and religious significance—Ayodhya—and then travelled by road to Varanasi. The BJP's point was by then clear: Modi, despite being from Gujarat, would be the new face of the party's UP representation, as had been the case with Atal

Bihari Vajpayee, who represented Lucknow in the Lok Sabha five times although he originally hailed from Madhya Pradesh.

No doubt the BJP was clever in fielding Modi from Varanasi as the city offered an ethos where the lines between religion, politics and culture could be redrawn to bring it electoral benefits. In fact, this is what Modi did when he visited Varanasi as the Lok Sabha candidate of the saffron party and famously said: '*Na mai kahi aya hu, na mujhe kisi ne bulaya hai, mujhe to Ma Ganga ne bulaya hai*' (Neither have I come anywhere, nor has anyone called me; I have been called here by Mother Ganga). Declaring that cleaning the Ganga was as much a political commitment as it was a religious duty, Modi pitched himself as the son of Kashi and promised to turn Varanasi into a Kyoto. This was not completely welcomed by the original Banarasis of the city. Given the deep religious and cultural history of Kashi, many like me wanted to know why it needed to be a Kyoto. Like Rome, perhaps, it surely needed modernization and infrastructure, but it definitely needed to retain its infinite spiritual charm and significance of being Lord Shiva's city. For me too, as for several Banarasis, Kashi was Kashi and Kyoto was Kyoto.

I travelled to the rural areas on the outskirts of the city and spoke to the villagers there. They were sceptical about the changes that might result in their lives with a national leader representing them.

The rhetorical appeal of Modi, however, worked spectacularly well for the BJP and he registered a thumping victory from Varanasi and his party surged to power in New Delhi. By the time Modi sought another term from Varanasi in 2019, it was already his bastion. Although there was discontent and disappointment among a few sections in the city this time, as they believed that the development promises for the city made during Modi's first term had not been fulfilled, they were firm that Modi deserved a second chance. The report card of development projects undertaken during Modi's first term suggested moderate progress. For sure, he had some fine achievements on the development front. The most noteworthy among them was India's first multi-modal terminal on the Ganga, with which Modi rewarded Varanasi in 2018.

It was in the same year that he inaugurated two important roads in the city: the 16.55-kilometre Varanasi Ring Road and the 7.25-kilometre Babatpur–Varanasi Road on NH-56. The Ring Road was hailed for relieving traffic on the Varanasi–Lucknow and Ayodhya–Varanasi highways. The Babatpur–Varanasi highway is being touted as the gateway to Varanasi. He also inaugurated the ambitious Rs 339 crore Kashi Vishwanath corridor project connecting the ancient Kashi Vishwanath temple to the ghats of the Ganga in December 2021, just ahead of the 2022 UP election. Ironically, Modi's pet Clean Ganga project failed to make good progress and continued to grab the headlines for its slow pace during his first term. But, despite these efforts, many political observers believed that Modi failed to deliver to Varanasi what he had originally promised in 2014. They were, in my opinion, quite right.

What they did not realize was that bastions in UP are created based on 'face value' and the rhetoric of development, and not exactly by means of actual development on the ground. Modi and the BJP knew that their relatively moderate performance on the development front was not going to disturb their prospects in Varanasi and Uttar Pradesh. And they were right. Modi swept Varanasi again in 2019, this time with bigger margins.

Back in 1952, almost 250 kilometres from Varanasi, Feroze Gandhi and Indira Gandhi were busy in the streets and roads of Rae Bareli. Those were the days when many Congress stalwarts were seeking constituencies to make their bid for the Lok Sabha. Feroze, after much consideration, had decided that he would contest from Rae Bareli. Since he was considered a close aide of the Nehrus, having married Indira in 1942, this town of Uttar Pradesh on the banks of the river Sai became a high-profile constituency during India's first general election.

This was perhaps just the first example of a particular region of eastern UP being represented by first-generation Congress heavyweights in the years immediately after Independence. Voters sent them to Parliament with great enthusiasm and hoped their representatives would bring development to their constituencies. And so they did, at least partially, through the charisma and authority they enjoyed in the political circles of New Delhi.

Thus, Feroze Gandhi, immediately after winning the election from Rae Bareli, had the entire district surveyed to explore the possibility of bringing in industries there. He was particularly committed to passing on the fruits of the Green Revolution to the region, and towards this end he set up a milk plant. In fact, it was believed that he himself brought in the cattle by aeroplane. The plant later improved its capacity and expanded. This was just one example of how Feroze Gandhi sought to transform Rae Bareli. During his time, the district saw holistic development in education and business, and in the construction of roads and water channels.

When Indira Gandhi took over Rae Bareli as her constituency, she too extended development plans to the district. Her biggest achievement was the establishment of the Indian Telephone Industries there, an outfit that once employed more than 12,000. The landscape of the city also transformed during her time as it acquired a massive telegraph office, a modern hospital, a degree college and other establishments. Her impact on the popular imagination of Rae Bareli was quite remarkable, and for years Indira Gandhi's name remained synonymous with development in the district.

In the post-Emergency years, Rae Bareli appeared to have been betrayed. Its reputation as a model district and industrial hub received a huge setback, and her assassination in 1984 further contributed to its decline. Many of the factories set up during her time—such as Concepta Cables Ltd, National Switch Gears, National Textiles Mills, UP State Spinning Mill, Mittal Fertilizer, UP Tyres and Tubes—saw closures. Indian Telephone Industries also became a failed project as most of the ancillary factories of the company subsequently shut down.

In the small village of Hasanapur in Rae Bareli district, the most prominent outfit was a Modi carpet factory, widely talked about as the industrial project that would bring jobs to many. But with Indira Gandhi's death, the fortunes of the factory and of Hasanapur, which lay on the highway connecting Lucknow and Rae Bareli, declined.

This is typical of India. Once a big leader loses an election or dies, the bastion created by the leader using his or her clout collapses and the people of the area suffer. UP in this regard had been no different.

The story of Amethi, another political bastion, is not very different. This constituency has seen the biggest Congress names—Sanjay Gandhi, Rajiv Gandhi, Sonia Gandhi and Rahul Gandhi—represent it. Sanjay Gandhi developed Jagdishpur, a small town in the constituency, as an industrial hub, and Rajiv Gandhi too nurtured it. During their time, firms like Bharat Heavy Electricals Ltd (BHEL) and Indo-Gulf Fertilizers opened units in Amethi, but after Rajiv Gandhi's demise most of the units closed down because they could not procure raw materials. It is widely believed that Rahul Gandhi's historic defeat in the 2019 general election from here was because he had not revived Amethi as an industrial hub. I have already written earlier in this book about my 2019 election coverage of Amethi, when I discovered that Rahul Gandhi was in serious trouble in his constituency, where Smriti Irani had become the new 'insider' for the people. Their complaint was that Rahul was rarely to be seen there.

The Etawah district of Uttar Pradesh is another political bastion that has gained a lot of media attention over the years. The reason is Saifai, the native village of Samajwadi Party patriarch Mulayam Singh Yadav. Saifai most famously hit the headlines in 2014, when Bollywood stars Salman Khan and Madhuri Dixit performed at the Saifai Mahotsav, the annual gala affair of the Samajwadi

Party. The event was organized in the wake of the communal riots in Muzaffarnagar in Uttar Pradesh, and both Salman Khan and Madhuri Dixit were condemned for participating in the musical extravaganza.

While this Bollywood presence in Saifai surprised many outside UP, it was hardly shocking for anyone who had seen the transformation of this small village of barren wetlands into a landscape of huge structures under the Yadavs. In fact, Chandgiram stadium, where the Saifai Mahotsav was held, was one of the reasons for Saifai remaining in the headlines in the national media for years. The stadium, named after Haryana wrestler Chandgiram, was inaugurated by Mulayam Singh Yadav in 2003 when he was chief minister. The fact that he himself had been a wrestler before he joined full-time politics, and that the majority of the wrestlers in western UP were Yadavs, made this stadium a powerful symbol denoting Yadav dominance in the region.

The makeover of Saifai went hand in hand with Mulayam Singh Yadav's ascent in politics. The son of Saifai first became chief minister in 1989. Among the first few significant things he did for Saifai was to make it the district headquarters. He ensured uninterrupted twenty-four-hour electricity supply in the village and went on to establish the Grameen Aur Vigyan Evam Anusandhan Sansthan, a medical institute fashioned after Delhi's All India Institute of Medical Sciences, in Saifai during his third stint as chief minister in 2003. This was also the time when he established the Master Chandgiram Sports Complex.

But the most transformative phase for the village began in 2012, when Akhilesh Yadav, son of Mulayam Singh Yadav and a postgraduate from the University of Sydney in Australia, spearheaded the Samajwadi Party to victory in the assembly elections. In contrast to Mulayam's anti-English and anti-computer stance, Akhilesh was committed to giving the party a modernist outlook. He could play football, hockey and cricket and appreciate the music of Guns N' Roses, Bon Jovi, Bryan Adams and Metallica. I remember how he carried an iPhone with him and became the darling of the New Delhi media during the 2012 election campaign. This was a drastic generational shift in the leadership of the decades-old Samajwadi Party that I was witnessing—from a party whose chief was a village wrestler to a party whose chief was now an English-speaking young man who listened to rock music and could bat and bowl on the cricket ground.

Soon the village of Saifai became the object of this shift. The Akhilesh Yadav government left no stone unturned to give the village a global and cosmopolitan touch. While it carried out several beautification and infrastructural works in Saifai, to me the most revealing project it undertook was the international cricket stadium on the Major Dhyan Chand Sports College campus. The stadium gained popularity for its high-class modern facilities, its seating capacity of over 40,000, an all-weather swimming pool and a multi-purpose hall. In 2018, when I visited the Melbourne cricket ground, the biggest in Australia, I realized to my surprise that the new one in Saifai was an exact replica of it. The reason, of course, was Akhilesh Yadav's exposure to cricket in Australia during his postgraduate studies days. Clearly, he wanted Saifai to have a similar cricket ground.

Another 'import' of Mulayam's was his signature cycle tracks which had coloured micro-surfacing with bitumen on the lines of those in the Netherlands. Today, Saifai stands as a perfect example of how political bastions in Uttar Pradesh are transformed into hubs of grand and huge structures as a result of the channelling of huge funds by their political patrons. Saifai has everything—a medical university, a full-fledged stadium, colleges for men and women, hostels for them, and an airstrip which is used by all political parties for campaigning. Yet, it has failed to create what can truly be considered a model of development for entire western UP.

The story of the state capital, Lucknow—the City of Nawabs, as it is called—has been equally telling. The city was represented by former prime minister Atal Bihari Vajpayee for five consecutive terms, and it was during his time as prime minister that Lucknow witnessed some of its monumental works of development, which changed the face of the city in the late 1990s and early 2000s.

Fondly referred to as Atalji by the commoners of Lucknow, Vajpayee was first elected as a parliamentarian from Lucknow in 1991. This was just the beginning of coalition politics in Uttar Pradesh, and leaders like Mulayam Singh Yadav and Mayawati were emerging on the political map of the state. But Vajpayee's position in Lucknow remained intact. By 1996, he was a stalwart figure in national politics, and Lucknow became the most keenly watched constituency in the nation.

The charisma of Vajpayee delivered the BJP some of its most famous victories in the state capital in the 1996, 1998 and 1999 general elections.

It was clear to the electorate of Lucknow that they were sending the prime minister of India to Parliament, and they were proven right when the BJP-led NDA formed the government in 1999 and Vajpayee took oath as prime minister. The fortunes of Lucknow were now to take a sharp turn for the better. The laying of Lucknow's first ring road, Shaheed Path, was a great gift to Lucknow that Vajpayee envisioned in 2001. This 24-kilometre peripheral highway decongested the roads of the state capital in a big way and still stands as Vajpayee's most significant legacy in the city.

But this was not all that Vajpayee did for Lucknow, recalls Sharat Pradhan, senior journalist and a long-time observer of UP politics. He says Vajpayee was equally concerned about grassroots issues at the micro level. He got a modern sewage treatment plant set up in the capital. It was during his term that the lanes and bylanes of the walled city, and its drainage and sanitation, were drastically improved. Pradhan also recalls how Vajpayee opened the doors for employment in the Middle East for the Muslim community in the city during his term as external affairs minister in the Janata Party government. Moves like this cast Vajpayee as a moderate in the right-wing politics of the Sangh—and were one of the reasons why he was never seen as anti-Muslim.

Through his charisma and vision, Vajpayee transformed Lucknow in many significant ways, but then the NDA was ousted from power in 2004. Though Vajpayee retained Lucknow with decent margins, he could no longer work for the city with the same zeal and enthusiasm. Most of the developmental works were taken over by his protégé Lalji Tandon, but by then Lucknow was already about Mulayam Singh Yadav and Mayawati. The biggest modernizing project in the city in the post-Vajpayee years came in the form of the Lucknow Metro. It was the Akhilesh Yadav government that launched the construction of this hi-tech public transport facility in 2014. Though the project remained controversial with debates over its utility and for its hasty implementation on the ground, it changed the landscape of the city decisively. The first stretch of the Lucknow Metro was inaugurated in September 2017 by Rajnath Singh, the parliamentarian from the city at that time, and it was termed as a historic day for the state capital.

Mayawati's flagship—and most ambitious—project, the Lucknow–Agra Expressway, which was inaugurated in 2012, also proved to be a game-changer for the city in the post-Vajpayee years, as it facilitated much faster and newer networks for road transport between New Delhi and Lucknow.

But the post-Vajpayee years for the city were not simply about the Lucknow Metro or the Lucknow–Agra Expressway. There was another big Mayawati connection to the development story of Lucknow. This connection emerged most revealingly in 2019, when India's apex court heard a 2009 lawsuit filed by two lawyers alleging that Mayawati had diverted huge public funds for building statues and parks to further her own political interests. The court's comment that Mayawati should pay back the public money spent on these projects was splashed on the front pages of newspapers, and there was again a huge debate over her development strategy for cities like Lucknow and Noida.

There was hardly any doubt that the Dalit memorials built during the many periods of her time as chief minister had only symbolic value for the city. The large statues of B.R. Ambedkar, Gautam Buddha, Birsa Munda, Jyotiba Phule and Kabir, apart from those of Kanshi Ram and Mayawati herself, stood in the middle of Lucknow as dominant spectacles of Mayawati's rise in Uttar Pradesh. She came under severe criticism, especially for installing her own statues in the state capital using public funds. It was indeed the first instance in India's political history of a living leader trying to immortalize herself by installing her own statues in public places. The memorials had fountains and stupas, meditation centres and exhibition areas in order to attract the common people. Currently in Lucknow, at least sixty-four elephant statues flank the Ambedkar Park next to the Gomti river, a reminder of the legacy left behind by Mayawati.

The real development failure for Mayawati was, however, not Lucknow. Her investment of huge sums in public parks and statues in the city became especially questionable in light of the plight of other regions of the state during her time. And nothing illustrated this better than the Bundelkhand region of the state. Situated along the south-western edge of UP, Bundelkhand has been one of the most backward regions of north-central India. The region remained insulated from the larger development schemes in the state as a result of its distinct geography. The ravines in the region provided cover to dacoit gangs moving on foot, and their influence subdued the life of the people here for years and years. Until the late 1980s perhaps, the Congress had considerable sway in Bundelkhand but, afterwards, the BSP, SP and BJP started making inroads into the region. Since OBCs and Dalits formed a majority of the population in the region, it was not very surprising that these parties became the choice of the electorate here in the 1990s.

But whether it was Mayawati's BSP or any other political party in power, the story of Bundelkhand throws light on the questionable use of *sarkari* packages awarded for the development of certain regions. The money is mostly spent in a corrupt manner, resulting in real development taking a backseat. To date, Bundelkhand serves as the worst example in UP of the diversion of such funds. Over Rs 1,800 crore was sanctioned for the period 2009–15 for the development of the region, yet one cannot see any sustainable change here.

The stakes for Mayawati and the BSP here suddenly rose during the 2007 assembly election, when the party won 14 of the 19 seats from the region. It was during this time that Bundelkhand became a hot-spot for the national media, as it emerged as a prospective political battleground for all the major players in UP. Rahul Gandhi, then Congress MP from Amethi, had famously alleged large-scale corruption in the development schemes going on in Bundelkhand. His direct attack on the Mayawati government for looting Rs 7,000 crore—the package awarded by the Centre for the development of the region—made headlines in 2008 and initiated a fierce war of words between the Congress and the BSP. Mayawati too hit back at the Congress, calling the Centre's special package for the region insufficient and demanding a 'special area' incentive package.

Both parties also locked horns over the issue of statehood for Bundelkhand. While the BSP said it was the duty of the central government to make Bundelkhand a separate state, the Congress passed the ball to the BSP, emphasizing that the state government should first pass a resolution in this regard. In fact, throughout her term as chief minister, Mayawati kept backing demands for statehood for Bundelkhand. Dividing the large state into smaller and more manageable ones was one of the crucial pre-election strategies for the 2012 assembly election for the BSP. But, as the outcome of the election demonstrated, this promise could not neutralize the disenchantment with the Mayawati government among the electorate in many pockets of UP, and it ultimately lost power to the Samajwadi Party.

Amidst all this politics over it, Bundelkhand itself continued to slump to new historic lows. The region continued to be an area where many farmers committed suicide because of their inability to pay back bank loans. News reports pointed out that neither Mayawati's regime nor Congress's famous loan waiver scheme launched in the run-up to the 2009 general election could bring respite to the farmers of the region. In fact, the budgetary allocations of the Mayawati-led BSP government painted the most accurate picture of the false promises it had made for the development of the Bundelkhand region. In 2010, the BSP government passed a supplementary budget of Rs 1,500 crore, out of which Rs 500 crore was allocated for Mayawati's pet statues project, while only Rs 10 crore was allocated for the drought-hit Bundelkhand region. This was just one story of how successive regimes in UP betrayed Bundelkhand.

The argument that UP needs to be split into many states—following the formation of Uttarakhand—arises from the lack of holistic development in the state. Better employment opportunities and better grassroots economics will ensure that the people of the state are not forced to leave it in such large numbers as they do now to look for work in other parts of India.

8

BJP Is Ram Bharose

If there is one issue for the BJP since its inception in 1980 that it has benefited from, both by keeping it alive or ignoring it depending on the political exigencies of the day, it is Ram Janmabhoomi. The deftness of the BJP and the Sangh in handling this issue is best illustrated by the rise of Atal Bihari Vajpayee, the party's most popular face, in the period following the demolition of the Babri Masjid.

It was not a very pleasant situation that the BJP leaders who had gathered at Palampur in the Himalayan foothills on 11 June 1989 found themselves in. They were discussing revival plans for the party. The BJP's representation in the Lok Sabha had been reduced to two in the latest general election, and the objective of their meeting was to come up with an issue that could haul it out of its existential crisis in national politics and pose a formidable challenge to the Congress and other opposition parties. The national executive of the BJP knew that the party was not a major player in the power politics of the country and that it needed a charismatic idea to push. It desperately needed to project itself as a responsible and trustworthy party, as accommodating as the Congress but less chaotic, and ready to take up the reins of the nation. It was time to take a final call on its future, which looked completely dark at the time of the Palampur meeting.

At this point, the political brilliance of party president L.K. Advani came into play. In a rather unconventional move, he appealed for the demarcating line between religion and politics to be removed and declared the BJP's official support to the Ram Janmabhoomi campaign being carried out by the VHP and other saffron outfits. It was this 'new politics' of Advani and the BJP that was to make the saffron party a major player in the politics of the Hindi heartland and subsequently in the politics of the country.

Undoubtedly, the Ram Janmabhoomi movement was at the heart of the new politics the BJP sought to champion from Palampur to shore up its political fortunes. By no means was this politics entirely new for Uttar Pradesh and the country. The erstwhile Jana Sangh had used sectoral and religious sentiments during elections on many occasions, and the Congress campaign in the 1984 general election in the aftermath of Indira Gandhi's assassination too had religious underpinnings. But nowhere in the distant past had religious issues been used so blatantly by a political party to enhance its electoral performance. The Palampur resolution of the BJP was the first move by any political party in post-Independence India that openly made a religious campaign part of its politics.

But what puzzled every political observer was the question of why the party had kept itself aloof from Ram Janmabhoomi affairs politically till 1989, and why it suddenly aligned with the VHP and the RSS on the temple issue that year. The answer to this question was perhaps very simple, says author and political observer Hemant Sharma. For the BJP, it was purely a strategic and timely move. By 1989, the VHP was already very vocal on the Ram Janmabhoomi issue. In February 1989, it had announced at its Dharam Sansad that a *bhoomipujan* ceremony would be held at the temple site on 9 November 1989. The extensive groundwork for the campaign was also planned. The Congress too was claiming its stake in the movement under the leadership of Rajiv Gandhi. Clearly, the Ram Janmabhoomi issue had become somewhat of a mass movement by 1989. The BJP was keenly aware of all these developments. So, by 1989, the Ram Janmabhoomi controversy had become an intensely discussed national issue that no political party could dare to overlook, Sharma writes in his book *Ayodhya: A Battleground.*

The overtly political undertone of the resolution confirmed that the BJP was all set to cash in on the issue. The party articulated its demands in the Ayodhya matter clearly in its resolution:

> Bharatiya Janata Party's national working committee is serious on the ongoing Ram Janmabhoomi dispute. The party is worried about the insensitive and indifferent attitude of political parties, especially that of Congress, towards the issue and about the betrayal to the majority population of the country which is Hindus. The party believes that according to all the available evidence, Mughal emperor Babur came to Ayodhya in 1528. He got all temples demolished around the area that is believed to be Lord Ram's birthplace. Babur got

> a mosque built there. Since then, Hindus have been waiting for reconstruction of a temple there, which they consider very holy.[17]
>
> During the war of independence in 1857, Muslims had agreed to the claims of Hindus on Ram Janmabhoomi, but the English played the divide and rule politics and the matter got worsened. Although despite all this, the efforts of making Muslims understand that they must drop their claim on this land and respect sentiments of Hindus continued. Even then the land got stuck in a long legal battle. BJP believes that this is a conflict a court cannot resolve.
>
> Courts can resolve disputes over posts and ownership. But a court cannot pass judgement on whether Babur actually attacked Ayodhya, got the temple demolished and built a mosque in its place. Even when a court has given a verdict on such matters, it has never been able to undo history's barbarity.[18]

The explicit terms in which the BJP warned the courts not to interfere in the matters of faith and sentiment of the Hindu community were a clear indication of the aggressive yet tactical stance that the party was increasingly going to take to woo the electorate. It was clearly a tactical position as the party knew from the very beginning that the matter would certainly go to the courts for settlement. It also knew that sooner or later the courts would issue directions in the matter, which would have to be followed by all political parties.

In fact, that's exactly what happened, especially in the Vajpayee era, when the party took a U-turn on the matter, consistently saying it would go by the court order on Ram Janmabhoomi even if it was against the party's original position on the issue. Such tactical flexibility on the BJP's part allowed it to flip-flop on the Ayodhya matter on several occasions. This has been discussed at the end of this chapter.

In terms of appeal and scope, the Ayodhya issue was unmatched. A vote for the BJP would be a step towards the restoration of the temple at Ram's precise birthplace. It was an astoundingly simple call and it worked almost immediately for the party. From two Lok Sabha seats in 1984, the BJP went on to reap a dream harvest of 86 in the election that took place in December 1989. This was the first taste of success for the party, and it had huge implications not only for the party but also for the entire country.

VHP and Sangh strategists had the answer to the key question as to why Ayodhya and the Ram Janmabhoomi movement were chosen by them to agitate for instead of Kashi and Mathura: their choice would enable the political transformation of the BJP on a large scale across the country. And so it did. As Hemant Sharma explains, there were no prayers being offered by Hindus in Ayodhya at the temple site, and this fact was potent enough for Hindu sentiments to align in favour of the BJP. And, as I myself observed in the 1990s, this surely triggered a new wave of right-wing politics in India.

At this juncture, the Congress party and the Rajiv Gandhi government at the Centre were losing ground in UP as well as in national politics, as mentioned before. The historic defeat of the party in the 1989 general election proved to be very crucial for the BJP, and for the VHP and RSS too. These outfits were now championing the cause of Ram Janmabhoomi more aggressively and in different parts of the country, apart from just UP. This was the golden opportunity for the BJP to project itself as a serious stakeholder in the Ayodhya movement. While in the mid-1980s the party leadership was not sure whether they would completely align with the movement for political gains, by the 1990s, with the defeat of its key rival, the Congress, the BJP had come to a clear understanding that only the Ayodhya issue could bring it into the mainstream of Indian politics, which had clearly been dominated by the Congress until the 1980s. As I have mentioned earlier, the party's Palampur resolution was the first clear sign of this realization, and its victory haul of 86 seats in the 1989 general election was, in many ways, strong confirmation of the success of this purely tactical shift.

But the chief strategists in the party were still worried about what its future course of action should be. There was talk in the party as to how it could seize the Janmabhoomi opportunity to maximize matters to its own political advantage. From the party's point of view, these concerns were valid to some extent. While it was true that the party by then had associated itself with the Ram Janmabhoomi movement officially, which had handsomely rewarded the party in the 1989 general election, it still lacked big faces that could be easily identified with the Ayodhya movement. All the big names of the movement until then had belonged to either the VHP or RSS. The party now wanted to create the perception that Ayodhya was not an issue that it had simply borrowed from the VHP but one that had always belonged to the BJP.

Here again, BJP president L.K. Advani came up with an idea that would, almost immediately, make him and the saffron party a household name across the country. While the VHP and RSS had already declared a 'kar seva' in Ayodhya, Advani managed to capture the headlines in September 1990 when he announced his plan to go on a pad yatra from Somnath to Ayodhya to educate people about the Ram Janmabhoomi movement. This was an ambitious campaign, the sole purpose of which was to further consolidate the BJP's grip on the Ayodhya issue. Advani discussed it with Pramod Mahajan, who had by then become one of the chief strategists of the party. Mahajan, with his penchant for flashy ideas, turned the pad yatra into a rath yatra. A Toyota mini-bus was decorated to look like a rath, with a high platform for Advani to sit on. Pramod Mahajan himself told me in his typical brazen style that he had always thought that while raising sentimental issues close to the heart for Hindus, the BJP must also look 'modern', and therefore the Toyota idea would work very well.[19]

The rath yatra was a masterstroke by Advani and Mahajan as it enabled the BJP to catalyse and capitalize on a chain of events. The rath became a powerful mobilizer for the party, with people across the country welcoming it with drums and bells. In some cities people even smeared the dust from its wheels on their foreheads. Throughout the journey, Advani was presented with an assortment of arms, including glittering *sudarshan chakras,* which he would swirl around his index finger, much to the delight of the crowd.

The rath yatra was another game changer for the BJP after its adoption of the Ram Janmabhoomi issue, in the sense that Advani chose Somnath as the starting point of the yatra. Since the Shiv temple at Somnath had been the reference point in the BJP's Hindutva discourse on Muslim aggression, the rath yatra contextualized Ayodhya along the same historical legacy of 'Muslim atrocities on Hindu places of worship'.

The outcome of Advani's rath yatra was far-reaching. There was, of course, communal backlash in the states of Uttar Pradesh, Karnataka, Andhra Pradesh and Gujarat, and Advani was even arrested in Samastipur on 23 October 1990 on the orders of chief minister of Bihar Lalu Prasad Yadav before he could reach in time for the kar seva at Ayodhya on 30 October. On 23 October, Uttar Pradesh too witnessed a deadly clash between the kar sevaks, who were gathering in huge numbers in Ayodhya, and the police. But the rath yatra had achieved the objective of providing force and visibility to the Ram Janmabhoomi issue. Though questions were raised as to whether Advani's audacious rath yatra had been able to create the greatest mass movement of post-Independence times in India, it was widely believed that his tour was a spectacular success in large parts of north and west India.

However, the real test for the BJP came in 1991, when the party registered a thumping victory in the UP assembly election and Kalyan Singh, a Lodh leader, was sworn in as chief minister. Hindu sentiment over the Ayodhya issue was at its peak then and it was believed that the BJP had been awarded a mandate in UP simply to facilitate the construction of a Ram temple in Ayodhya. Kalyan Singh too wasted no time in spreading the message that his party was committed to constructing a Ram temple in Ayodhya. On 25 June 1991, he visited Ayodhya along with his MLAs and reiterated his party's position that the temple would be built at the site where the *shilanyaas* had happened. The UP government went on to acquire 2.77 acres of the disputed land for the construction of the temple and even started to build a '*Ram deewar*' around the site, violating the 25 October 1991 orders of the Allahabad High Court, which barred any kind of permanent construction on the disputed site.

The next few months were the most turbulent in the state's—and the nation's—politics. Amidst repeated violations of the court's order, meetings between different stakeholders in the Ram Janmabhoomi matter and clashes between the central and UP governments, thousands and thousands of supporters of the VHP, BJP and Shiv Sena demolished the Babri Masjid on 6 December 1992. The state and the nation exploded, and a bloodbath followed in several parts of the country. Though, prior to the demolition, the Kalyan Singh government had repeatedly assured the Supreme Court that only a symbolic kar seva would be allowed and the state government would provide adequate security to the Babri Masjid, the demolition couldn't be stopped. Hemant Sharma has vividly described the happenings at the site that day in one of his books:

> I could see the violent nature of these Kar Sevaks from 9:30 in the morning, even though it had been decided the previous night that the Kar Seva will only be symbolic. In July's Kar Seva, there was a platform made at the conflicted site. At the chosen auspicious time, priests were supposed to clean up the area and begin the creation of a symbolic pillar. Volunteers were supposed to shower flowers and water here. So according

to plan, at 10:00 a.m., there were about a hundred and fifty priests sitting there, ready with all that was needed.

Just then the Additional Superintendent of Police (ASP) Anju Gupta reached the spot along with Lal Krishna Advani, Ashok Singhal and Murli Manohar Joshi. Kar Sevaks got aggressive after seeing L.K. Advani. They thought he had come there to suspend the Kar Seva once again, and so they got violent, broke barricading and tried to get to the platform where rituals were to be performed.

Looking at the aggression of the mob, the police became active and tried to push the mob out. But by then, some Kar Sevaks had crossed the barricading and had reached the platform. They pushed Advani and Joshi. Ashok Singhal tried to control the situation. But nobody was even recognizing them at that point.

Close to the conflicted site and opposite the sanctorum was Manas Bhawan. This was a religious rest house. From its roof, the entire expanse of sixty-five acres was clearly visible. The Vishwa Hindu Parishad had been in charge of making journalists sit here. About a dozen cameras were placed on the roof. On the second floor, there were cameras of Intelligence Bureau. The entire scene appeared saffron in color and all we could see was an outburst of rage. Along with the police, there were RSS's volunteers, the Ganveshdhari who were trying to control the mob.

By 11.00 in the morning, the dormant volcano started erupting. The mob of Kar Sevaks started trying to break down the barricading again. They even captured the roof of Manas Bhawan, where we were standing. We felt that the roof would collapse. Fearing this, we came downstairs and went to the roof of Sita Rasoi, which was about a hundred yards away from the conflicted structure. The police control room was also on the same roof. This was the safest place for me I felt since everything was visible from here and all the information was also accessible.

The situation was out of control in the eyes of the administration. It was in control for Kar Sevaks. But overall, the situation did get out of control. No one was ready to listen to anything. Advani was requesting the Kar Sevaks from the Ram Katha stage to return. He was also scolding them. Seeing all his appeals go in vain, Ashok Singhal took over the mic. He announced that the conflicted structure was not a mosque, but a temple and therefore Kar Sevaks should not damage it. For the sake of Ram Lalla, they should come down. When this also had zero impact, Ashok Singhal and Mahant Nrityagopal Das got off the stage and walked towards the structure. Everyone respected them. But the frenzied mob misbehaved with them as well. Both returned feeling hopeless. Just then someone gave the information that the Kar Sevaks on the dome were from South India. The top leader of the Sangh, H.V. Sheshadri, appealed in all four languages of South India one by one. He said that breaking the structure is not part of the Sangh's or VHP's agenda. 'You all please get down.' But no one was ready to listen to him either. After some time, such appeals could not be heard. It came to be known later that someone had cut the wire of the mic.[20]

While this description makes for a telling first-hand account of the sequence of events that led to the demolition of the Babri Masjid on 6 December 1992, it also tells us how emotionally charged the masses were at the time of this incident. As happens in every act of public violence, it is almost impossible to control a mob at the height of its frenzy, and that is exactly what happened in Ayodhya that day. With the demolition of the structure, it mattered little who was responsible for the circumstances. A feeling of shock, instead, enveloped everyone, including the BJP, clearly the key face of the Ayodhya movement. So intense was this feeling of shock that L.K. Advani later went on to regret the demolition of the structure.

What followed after 6 December 1992 was also equally telling for the light it threw on the vexed relations between the chief political parties in the country and their attitude to the incident. They had been in constant touch with each other in the lead-up to the incident and had left no stone unturned to exploit the issue to their own political advantage. To get a sense of how Ayodhya became the object of a power tussle between the major political players of the time, the incessant phone calls to 7 Race Course Road, the prime minister's residence in the national capital, could be considered one indication. It was highly unlikely that a phone call would not be answered at such a time at the prime minister's residence. But it became clear only after some time that the phone calls were deliberately not being answered.

These calls were from B. Satya Narayan Reddy, governor of Uttar Pradesh, who wanted to discuss with Prime Minister P.V. Narasimha Rao whether or not he should accept the resignation of UP chief minister Kalyan Singh in the wake of the Babri

Masjid demolition that had happened just a few hours ago. With severe criticism coming his way from all political quarters, including his own, Rao refused to talk to the governor. He was upset with Reddy for having failed to anticipate the demolition of the masjid, and for sending misleading reports to New Delhi instead. Only three days before the demolition, Reddy had written a letter to Rao assuring the Centre that the situation in Ayodhya was under control and that there was no need to dismiss the state government.

Such a trust deficit between New Delhi and Lucknow was typical of the all-round trust deficit obtaining at the time. If Rao was upset with the UP governor for misleading the Centre by saying that matters were under control, the chief minister of UP was displeased with the VHP leadership for not disclosing their 'actual' plans at Ayodhya. Kalyan Singh had been assured by several VHP leaders involved in the negotiations going on for settlement of the temple issue that there would be only symbolic kar seva at Ayodhya and that the Babri structure would not be touched. But the high-voltage drama in the city on what began as a pleasant Sunday morning that 6 December had left him stunned. How could the VHP keep the person who headed the state aloof from a plan of such extraordinary implications?

So, every party was trying to extract something for itself from the movement. At stake were not just ideologies but on-the-ground benefits they would get to reap. If for the BJP and its affiliates, the VHP and RSS, it was about making Ram a symbol of their ascendancy in national politics, for the ruling Congress regime it was mostly about stopping the BJP from getting credit for the movement. Many of the party's moves during this period were guided by its anxiety over the BJP's rising influence in the Hindi heartland. The grand old party, first under the leadership of Rajiv Gandhi and then under Narasimha Rao's, made every effort to ensure that the Congress too remained in the game of temple politics. The country was in a situation so helpless it could do little but just mourn its fate.

For the Congress, the chase for Ayodhya, and consequently the Hindu vote, had started during Rajiv Gandhi's time. But the power politics around Ayodhya was played by all political parties in the country, sometimes subtly, sometimes in an open manner. Thus, when V.P. Singh became prime minister with outside support from the BJP after the Congress's defeat in the 1989 election, Ayodhya naturally became a tricky situation for him to handle. His coalition government at the Centre was supported by the BJP, which was now aggressively championing the Ram Janmabhoomi movement to pander to Hindu sentiments. Its support to the V.P. Singh government not only ensured the BJP a stake in the power politics of New Delhi but also simultaneously ensured that the party could now bargain with V.P. Singh on Ayodhya, according to its convenience. This layer of power politics around Ayodhya was still understandable, as both V.P. Singh and the BJP had entered into a tactical deal—V.P. Singh was to run his government with support from the BJP and the BJP in turn got to bargain with V.P. Singh on Ayodhya.

But there was one more layer to this politics that was not very apparent, and it operated very subtly between Prime Minister

V.P. Singh and UP chief minister Mulayam Singh Yadav, who too was running a Janata Dal coalition government in the state. Ideally, this should have resulted in greater coordination between Singh and Yadav on Ayodhya; after all, they both represented a non-Congress-coalition, but that is where the politics of Ram Janmabhoomi movement proved itself complex and tricky. V.P. Singh and Mulayam Singh Yadav considered each other arch rivals, and this internal politics of the Janata Dal was also played through Ayodhya. Both repeatedly attacked each other on the issue and made sure that neither got a political edge in the situation. Thus, when V.P. Singh began talks with the *sant* community on Ayodhya, Mulayam Singh Yadav saw this as an attempt to provoke the *sants* against him. On the other hand, V.P. Singh thought Mulayam Singh Yadav was conspiring against his government by blocking his dialogue with the *sants* and the VHP. Hemant Sharma here reveals a very interesting incident:

> Once V.P. Singh told me that he had almost reached a compromise with the sants after talks with them. After that, Mulayam Singh got only those sants arrested who were involved in the talks. And not just that. To counter V.P. Singh's attempt at compromise, Mulayam Singh Yadav appointed Azam Khan, one of the members of the Babri Action Committee, to the UP cabinet. V.P. Singh in turn did not include Mulayam Singh Yadav in the three-member panel that he constituted to take the Ayodhya matter forward.

Clearly, the BJP's lobbying with the Janata Dal also exacerbated the Ayodhya problem. It is believed that the arrest of L.K. Advani during his rath yatra in Samastipur on 23 October 1990 was also masterminded by V.P. Singh as he did not want Mulayam Singh Yadav to get credit for Advani's arrest if it happened in UP. So, he persuaded Lalu Prasad Yadav, then chief minister of Bihar, to make the move. Though, by ordering police action on kar sevaks on the day of Advani's arrest in Ayodhya, Mulayam did manage to get an edge over V.P. Singh, who had to eventually resign from his post after the BJP withdrew support for his government. The Singh-led government lost the no-confidence motion by 146–342 votes in Parliament. This was another example of how powerful the Ayodhya issue was in the 1990s. It could topple a government almost overnight.

After V.P. Singh's departure, a Chandrashekhar-led breakaway section of the Janata Dal formed the government at the Centre with support from the Congress. Chandrashekhar too looked for a solution to the Ayodhya matter. During his brief tenure of four months at the Centre, he tried to bring the disputing parties face to face. Almost six rounds of talks were held under the supervision of Sharad Pawar, Bhairon Singh Shekhawat and Mulayam Singh Yadav, but then again the insecurity of the Rajiv Gandhi-led Congress came into play. The party withdrew support to the Chandrashekhar government, and it was rightly speculated that Rajiv Gandhi did not want him to take the credit for solving the Ayodhya issue.

The role of P.V. Narasimha Rao, another prime minister of the Congress, also became questionable after the demolition of the structure. Who was at the control panel when the Babri structure was demolished by hundreds of kar sevaks in Ayodhya on 6 December 1992? Who was to be held accountable for an incident that shook the conscience of the nation? These were the questions that surfaced when the Babri Masjid was demolished. Naturally, the onus of answering these questions fell on the Rao government. For sure, it is always the responsibility of a state government to maintain law and order in its territory. In this sense, the Kalyan Singh government had clearly failed. Kalyan Singh could not fulfil his commitment of securing the Babri structure, despite reassuring everyone many times before the demolition that he would. But the Ayodhya script was not written by the Kalyan Singh government alone.

At the time of the demolition, the Congress led by Prime Minister Rao was keeping a curious eye on the proceedings at Ayodhya. Rao's role in controlling the affairs of the campaign had unquestionably been crucial even before 6 December 1992. Just three days before, he had met key RSS functionaries, who had agreed that the structure would not be demolished, and that permission would be given only for a ceremony to be held outside the disputed area. Rajasthan chief minister Bhairon Singh Shekhawat and a few others were also present at the meeting. This meeting was part of the backdoor negotiations that were often mediated by former *Jansatta* editor, the late Prabhash Joshi. He played an instrumental role in bringing all the stakeholders of Ayodhya to the table several times during this period to work out a consensus. Interestingly, it was Prabhash Joshi who consistently conveyed to Kalyan Singh New Delhi's position on the Ayodhya issue during this period.

Such negotiations, in which the Centre's involvement was far from evident, clearly demonstrated that the affairs of temple politics were managed not by a single but multiple 'control panels'. In Lucknow, UP chief minister Kalyan Singh was in the driver's seat; in New Delhi it was Prime Minister P.V. Narasimha Rao who dictated the proceedings. This is not to forget that the Congress and BJP both remained in touch with the leadership of the RSS and VHP throughout.

This being the case, a clash between New Delhi and Lucknow was inevitable. It was indeed ironic that the matter of the deployment of central security forces in parts of UP became the chief issue in this clash. It all started when the Congress regime at the Centre sent a large contingent of security forces to UP fearing violence because of the large numbers of kar sevaks that had gathered in the Ayodhya–Faizabad area. The Kalyan Singh government hit back at the Centre saying the situation in UP was under complete control and that the Centre should immediately recall these forces. In a letter written just a week before the masjid demolition, Kalyan Singh accused the ruling Congress government of misusing its power and weakening the federal structure of the Constitution. He wrote that the forces were sent without the state government's consent and this was clearly against the structure of the Indian Constitution. What was perhaps most shocking in his letter was the allegation that Rapid Action Force commandos had been sent to terrorize the masses in Ayodhya and nearby areas. One incident cited in support of this was two central-force sub-inspectors threatening the police control room in Ayodhya.

If it was difficult to make sense of such a portrayal of the central security forces, things got even worse when the UP government sent information to the Centre, based on the Faizabad district magistrate's report, alleging that jawans were creating a ruckus in the red-light area of the city after getting drunk. The UP government also accused the paramilitary personnel deployed in the city of misconduct with women and sex workers. The charges against the central security forces did not end there. They were accused of power theft by the city's electricity department; the complaint was that their presence 'put pressure' on transformers, putting them in danger of burning or exploding.

Needless to say, the charges against India's central security forces were of a very serious nature. This was one of the rarest occasions in Indian politics when security forces had found themselves at the receiving end of politics played between the Centre and a state. Kalyan Singh's letter and the UP government reports sent to New Delhi branded them as lumpens, thieves and looters blocking the construction of the Ram temple in the holy city of Hindus. Such was the power of politics played around Ayodhya that it painted one of the most reputed and respectable security forces of the country as notorious in the minds of thousands of people.

The Centre did not deliver a categorical reply to these charges against the security forces but asserted that the law and order situation in several parts of UP, including Ayodhya and Faizabad, was deteriorating. In his reply to Kalyan Singh's letter the day before the Babri Masjid was demolished, Home Minister S.B. Chavan warned the UP government about the large gathering of kar sevaks in Ayodhya. He even mentioned that many kar sevaks were buying *trishools* to attack the central forces with. Throughout his reply, Chavan's emphasis was on the inadequacy of security arrangements by the UP government and warned that kar sevaks entering Ayodhya in such large numbers could damage the Babri structure. The paramilitary forces, thus, should be sent to such places almost immediately to control the situation, Chavan wrote.

It was clear that the war of words between New Delhi and Lucknow reflected the efforts on the part of both to sing the Ayodhya song to their own tune. The Centre and the UP government each viewed the ground situation in Ayodhya differently. They calculated differently. For the Kalyan Singh government, it was almost impossible to restrict the number of kar sevaks who could enter Ayodhya and Faizabad. It did not want any interference from the Centre as it wanted to ensure that the party got all the credit for the symbolic kar seva. The central leadership of the Congress wanted to save its secular credentials while simultaneously making sure that the party never looked aloof from the Ram Janmabhoomi campaign.

One question that remained unanswered amidst this enmity between the Centre and state was how kar sevaks in such large numbers were able to gather in Ayodhya and nearby areas. For sure, devotees had always been visiting Ayodhya and Faizabad from all over the country. At the time of the demolition, almost half of the states in the country were run by the Congress. How did the Congress-ruled states allow kar sevaks to cross their borders and gather in UP in such large numbers? Does it not hint at dual strategies that the Congress regime might have chalked out to exploit the Ayodhya issue to its advantage? There is hardly any doubt that state governments are fully capable of restricting the mobilization of masses in their territories. Had this happened, one of the most horrific incidents of post-Independence India could have been avoided.

It was clear to me and many political observers of the time that the BJP was selling the Ram temple issue to voters to further its electoral fortunes, and during the run-up to the demolition it was doing this successfully. But after the demolition, the Ayodhya strategy did not translate into votes in ways the party had thought it would. In fact, to the surprise of all of us, the BJP slumped in elections in UP held shortly after the demolition. Hemant Sharma says this was because the construction of a Ram temple was no longer an issue for voters after the demolition of the Babri. Still, the party optimistically kept using the Ram Janmabhoomi issue over the years to keep it alive in the national imagination.

During the 1996 and 1998 general elections, the BJP reiterated its stand on the construction of a Ram temple at the disputed site in Ayodhya; in the 1999 election, the BJP-led NDA did not even mention Ayodhya in its manifesto. It was a tactical compromise to form a coalition government at the Centre. In 2004, the party even went against its original 1989 Palampur resolution, perhaps for the first time saying that it was in favour of a judicial verdict in the matter.

Many of the BJP's flip-flops on Ayodhya were part of the stark reality of coalition politics it found itself in. Atal Bihari Vajpayee had already emerged as the most acceptable face of a large non-Congress coalition, the NDA. Even during the early days of this alliance, as I looked at its government and its PMO closely as a reporter, it was clear to me that during the Vajpayee era the

Ayodhya issue had to be tactfully handled and never brought to a level where it could bring discomfort to any of the BJP's new partners in the larger coalition. This politics was directly the result of the BJP's thirteen-day-experiment in power, when its government collapsed and it could not hold on to office because many parties were not ready to support it. And this was when Vajpayee began to argue, both in and outside Parliament, that the BJP was not untouchable.

Against this background of Vajpayee's leadership and NDA politics, Ayodhya had to be dealt with political wisdom. For me as a journalist, this understanding came in March 2002, when the VHP-proposed *shila dan* turned out to be a damp squib. Never could the VHP recreate the old frenzy in Ayodhya again. In the second week of March, many journalists like me descended on Ayodhya for this *shila dan*. The entire country's focus was on Ayodhya and there was palpable tension both in Delhi and on the ground. As a reporter who covered the PMO, the sense I got was that nothing would be allowed to happen in Ayodhya that could embarrass the Vajpayee government. The government had a variety of key players to take along—ranging from the socialist George Fernandes to its own traditional Ram Janmabhoomi movement ally, the Shiv Sena—so a balance had to be maintained.

There were reporters and cameramen all over the place from both the national and international media. By now the most famous hotel in Faizabad, Shan-e-Awadh, was a melting pot of endless stories about how the government in Delhi was handling this. Reporting each day, I witnessed Ayodhya turn into a fortress, with security and paramilitary forces all over the place. The tension was so immense that I still clearly remember that in the middle of some live TV coverage, I was troubled by a group of young men chanting 'Jai Sri Ram', but soon they noticed the heavy presence of security forces all around and moved away. As 15 March, the declared date for the *shila dan*, approached, the city was virtually shut down. It was to be a symbolic ceremony, as had been promised in 1992 too.

But Vajpayee's PMO was not ready to take any chances. A special officer from the PMO, Shatrughan Singh, was sent to Ayodhya to ensure that nothing went out of the local administration's or the central government's control. The man at the centre of all this locally in Ayodhya was Ramachandra Das Paramhans, head of the Ram Janmabhoomi Nyas. Every evening, journalists would flock to him to know what would be happening next in Ayodhya. Paramhans conveyed to journalists that everything was fine. In more than one way, this was ironic, because in 1992 it was exactly the same kind of messages that were delivered to Prime Minister Narasimha Rao by right-wing leaders—like the famous 7.30 a.m. phone call Rao had made to Vinay Katiyar, president of the VHP youth wing Bajrang Dal, on 6 December 1992 asking if everything was under control and Katiyar had replied, yes, everything was fine. What happened next, as we all know, is history. So, there was bound to be tension in Faizabad and Ayodhya now too, with 15 March 2002 approaching.

Etched in my memory is a long, fearful walk from my OB van to the disputed site. Security men were perched on top of the houses lining the streets of Ayodhya, their pointed guns ready for any untoward situation that may arise. It was one of the scariest reporting assignments I had done, and I will forever remember that walk down the street with my cameraman. As I described earlier, Ayodhya was turning into a fortress, exactly as the footage broadcast during those days on television showed. Every nook and corner, lane and bylane, had massive security presence, and the message as I chatted with local policemen on duty was loud and clear—1992 would not be repeated.

Finally, on 15 March 2002, the *shila* was donated for the construction of the Ram temple at the *shila dan* ceremony held in the temple town. As expected, the chairman of the Ram Janmabhoomi Nyas, Mahant Ramachandra Das Paramhans, donated the *shila* to Vajpayee's emissary Shatrughan Singh at the Bada Sthan in Ayodhya. For the commissioner of the region, Anil Gupta, there was enormous pressure both from Lucknow and Delhi to maintain law and order that day. Finally, true to their stated position, Vajpayee and his administration made sure that the VHP programme could not recreate the old atmospherics.

The very next day, on 16 March 2002, Vajpayee strongly dismissed the VHP's claim that acceptance of the *shila dan* in Ayodhya the previous day did not in any way represent the government's in-principle approval for the Ram temple; it was clarified that the construction of the shrine could begin only if the Supreme Court favoured it. Vajpayee said in Parliament, 'We have made our position very clear. The issue of temple construction is pending before the court. If the court's verdict is in favour of Hindus, the construction of the temple would begin, otherwise not.' It was generally believed that Vajpayee's allies were happy and satisfied that during his government there was no revisiting of Ayodhya along the old lines.

As it happened, when the Supreme Court judgement on Ayodhya was finally delivered around 10.30 a.m. on 9 November 2019, I was in Lucknow again. Now it was the Narendra Modi government at the Centre. But the same Lucknow that I saw as a young boy, witnessing the work of kar sevaks all over the city in 1992, was virtually shut down. And there was no reaction at all to the judgement. Not just Lucknow, but the entire state of Uttar Pradesh and the country remained calm. Because for the nation it was eventually, as Vajpayee had said, an issue settled by the Supreme Court of India. By early evening that day, shops reopened in Lucknow and in a few hours life went back to normal, with one of the most tumultuous issues in UP and the country reaching some kind of closure. With the *bhoomipujan* for the Ram temple happening on 5 August 2020 during the coronavirus pandemic, it was an issue that had come a full circle in the BJP's political life.

9

The Switchers

In the Indian Political league, auctions do not happen in public as in the Indian Premier League in cricket, but the outcomes are more or less the same. Political players can change sides every political season, as per their own needs and the preferences of the 'bidding' parties. This is one aspect of Indian politics that has provided it great colour for decades. In fact, '*Aaya Ram Gaya Ram*' is an Indian term that was coined in Haryana to describe party-hopping politicians. But it is just as descriptive of politicians in any state in India, including, of course, Uttar Pradesh.

The herd movement of politicians from their own party to another—often a party with opposite ideological leanings—has always provided some melodramatic flavour to the politics of UP since the 1990s. In official parlance, they are termed 'defectors', but I prefer to call them 'switchers', awkward though it might sound. They are indeed switchers for me as their loyalties are never fixed. They simply shift their allegiance from one party to another, according to their own political convenience, but often referring to the call to change as the voice of their inner conscience. Such voices of 'inner conscience' have jolted the politics of UP frequently in the past and continue to do so even in an era marked by the rising dominance of the BJP in the state and in the country as a whole. While the trend of political stalwarts moving to rival camps just before or after the polls has consolidated in the politics of many states, in UP it has impacted political affairs in perhaps the most unprecedented and dramatic ways in all of the country.

Vijay Bahuguna, a former chief minister of the state and son of the late Congress veteran Hemvati Nandan Bahuguna, rebelled from the Congress and joined the BJP in 2016 along with his sister and another Congress stalwart from UP, Rita Bahuguna Joshi, just before the 2017 assembly election. It was common talk in Lucknow circles that Rita was not happy with former Delhi chief minister Sheila Dikshit being chosen as the party's chief ministerial face for UP. In fact, the Bahugunas were not the only lot to desert their 'parental' party. Around the same time, Swami Prasad Maurya and S.P. Singh Baghel left the BSP and joined the BJP; and Anil Rajbhar, a backward-caste leader, left the Samajwadi party and joined the BJP. At roughly the same time, Brajesh Pathak, a two-term BSP MP and a close-aide of Mayawati's, also hit the headlines when he joined the saffron brigade expressing his faith in the development agenda of Narendra Modi. They all ended their long-time associations with their original parties and were later rewarded handsomely by the BJP.

The case of BSP founding member R.K. Chaudhary is much more dramatic. He joined the SP in 2017, hoping he would become a major face of the party in the 2019 Lok Sabha election. But after the SP and BSP formed their historic pre-poll alliance, he left the SP and joined the Congress, which fielded him from

Mohanlalganj. A humiliating defeat in this constituency sent him back to the SP. This is a typical example of how switchers move across political parties and impact electoral calculations in UP. As the 2022 assembly election in the state draws near, this trend is only consolidating. The leaders are already assessing what in UP politics is often called '*hava ka rukh*'—or getting a sense of which way the wind is blowing.

But it was in the 1990s that the political climate of UP witnessed the winds of turbulent change most powerfully, and switchers were the architects of most of these upheavals. By that time, the country itself had witnessed some high-profile 'switcher' activity in national politics. The case of influential Jat leader Chaudhary Charan Singh leaving the Congress and creating his own party, the Bhartiya Kranti Dal, in 1967 was the most significant of them. The curious case of the independent MLA Gaya Lal from Haryana caused vast entertainment when, in 1967, he famously switched between the Congress and Vishal Haryana Party three times within a short span of a week, after which '*Aaya Ram Gaya Ram*' became an established phrase in political circles to describe all such dramatic cases of defection. It was again in Haryana that Janata Party leader and state chief minister Bhajan Lal convinced all his MLAs to join the Congress with him in 1980 despite their clear majority in the assembly. These cases are reminders that switchers were rising in the politics of the Hindi heartland even before the 1990s, when they became very active.

What happened in UP during the 1990s was, however, extraordinary in more ways than one. The end of Congress monopoly in that decade ushered in a new era of coalition politics in the state, where the practice of unseating the governments of rival parties with the help of switchers became so common that the state saw four chief ministers in a span of just six years between 1989 and 1995. One of the intriguing features of this period was the politicization of the office of the governor, recalls senior journalist Brajesh Shukla, who had observed UP politics closely throughout the 1990s. He says it was very common in those years for the chief minister of the state to meet the governor behind closed doors and convince him to dissolve the assembly. Often the decision to dissolve the assembly was taken overnight by the governor and coalition partners were left surprised.

This is exactly what Mayawati did on 1 June 1995, says Shukla. Amidst the differences between the BSP and SP over several issues in the coalition government headed by Mulayam Singh Yadav, Mayawati met then governor of Uttar Pradesh Motilal Vora and declared that her party was withdrawing support to the Mulayam Singh government. The very next day, SP and BSP supporters clashed with each other in the state guest house at Mirabai Marg in Lucknow. During the clash, Mayawati had to lock herself in a room for at least nine hours and was rescued only after L.K. Advani extended his party's support to the BSP.[21]

But in reality, Mayawati had already negotiated with the BJP, recalls Brajesh Shukla. We still believe that the BJP decided to support Mayawati after the guest house incident. But the fact is, both parties had already been exploring the possibility of an alliance backdoor, and only after they drew some sort of deal did Mayawati go to Raj Bhavan to announce withdrawal of support to the Mulayam Singh government, explains Shukla.

Such backdoor deals and negotiations destabilized the politics of UP in altogether new ways and forced the state to face fresh elections a number of times during the 1990s. The Mayawati government survived only for 137 days and the state went to the polls again in March 1996, and this began a new chapter of defections in the politics of the state. The splintered verdict in this election left the state in peril once again, and once again it was an opportunity for the switchers to exploit this tricky situation to their advantage. Thus, after much deliberations, BSP supremo Kanshi Ram and the BJP's L.K. Advani forged an alliance with a rotational formula, under which Mayawati was to be chief minister for six months, after which she was to relinquish office for Kalyan Singh. Neither the leaders of the United Front regime at Centre nor the Congress got wind of this extraordinary formula of power sharing. They even got Parliament to approve an extension to President's rule in the state. The governor, Romesh Bhandari, was already in favour of this, but the move by the BSP and BJP completely overturned the plan.

The coalition government of the BSP and BJP was riddled with problems from the very beginning. Kalyan Singh, a Lodh leader and a key face of the Ayodhya moment, was upset at the BJP high command's decision to forge an alliance with the BSP. He was a consistent opponent of the BSP–BJP tie-up and there was a prevalent belief in Lucknow circles that he was deliberately kept out of the negotiations between Advani, Vajpayee and Kanshi Ram. Realizing his displeasure, the central leadership sought to placate him by promising to make an effort to break the BSP in the next six months, reveals Brajesh Shukla. Mayawati was also aware of this intention from the day she was sworn in as chief minister under this agreement. Both partners clashed on several ideological issues too, says senior journalist Sharat Pradhan.

Immediately after Mayawati took over as CM, a war of words started between the BJP state unit leaders and Mayawati over the issue of Dalit protection. The massive bureaucratic reshuffle and Mayawati's district renaming spree also infuriated the BJP. Kalyan Singh was particularly unhappy over the bifurcation of his home district Aligarh, recalls Pradhan. His traditional constituency Atrauli fell in Aligarh, and the carving out of a new district, Mahamaya Nagar, from Aligarh was something that annoyed Kalyan Singh.

It was therefore inevitable that the alliance was not going to survive for very long. The first sign of a fallout between the BSP and BJP came when Mayawati completed her stint of six months as chief minister. Making unfriendly noises about the BJP, she reluctantly handed over charge to Kalyan Singh. But exactly after twenty-eight days, flaying the BJP for its anti-Dalit approach and actions, Mayawati pulled out of the alliance with the party on 19 October 1997. Sharat Pradhan recollects the key points of the five-page letter Mayawati sent to Governor Romesh Bhandari. Mayawati was primarily unhappy over Kalyan Singh's order to curb misuse of the SC Act. She also condemned Kalyan Singh for his large-scale transfer of senior bureaucrats and police officials of a Dalit background, Pradhan says.

No political pundit could have anticipated that the UP assembly was going to witness one of the biggest dramas in its political history in the upcoming days. When Mayawati withdrew support for the BJP, there were speculations that Governor Romesh Bhandari would dissolve the assembly. But in a surprise move, he decided to call a session of the state assembly on 21 October 1997 and asked Kalyan Singh to prove his majority in the assembly. Kalyan Singh had thirty-six hours to do so, and it was during these hours that Lucknow witnessed a dramatic turn of events. At around 6 p.m. on 20 October, fifteen Congress MLAs led by Naresh Agrawal and Gorakhpur's don-turned-politician Hari Shankar Tiwari approached the 14 Mall Road residence of speaker Keshari Nath Tripathi in twenty Tata Sumos and Ambassadors and asked for their recognition as Loktantrik Congress. By midnight, Tripathi was informed that the number of rebel MLAs had risen to twenty-two. Brajesh Shukla says all the rebel MLAs were corralled into a house in Lucknow.

But what was unfolding in the BSP party office in Lucknow was also something that shocked everyone, says Shukla. Mayawati was informed of a revolt in her party on 20 October 1997; seventeen legislators were alleging that they were imprisoned in the party headquarters. She rushed to the party office late that evening; there she was heckled by angry MLAs, following which she had to leave immediately. If Naresh Agrawal was leading the rebel MLAs in the Congress, Chaudhary Narendra Singh, a Kurmi leader, was at the helm of affairs in the BSP. Things were certainly slipping from Mayawati's hands, Brajesh Shukla recalls. By around midnight, Chaudhary Narendra Singh resigned as political adviser to BSP president Kanshi Ram. By then he had secured the support of twenty-four MLAs, but the split in the party could not materialize as the security guards in the party office blocked the gates by force. In Lucknow circles almost everyone knew who exactly was engineering these splits. The man behind these scenes was none other than Kalyan Singh, who was now eagerly waiting for the assembly session the next day.

21 October 1997 was the day of climax of all these developments for me and for many others of my fraternity who had been witnessing this incredible drama of tussle for power in the state capital. All the developments of the past thirty-six hours had happened behind the scenes, and now it was time for the stakeholders to face each other in the state assembly. They were bound to clash on the floor, and so they did, but in a manner that none of us could ever imagine. Immediately after the proceedings of the assembly started, Congress leader Pramod Tiwari, along with his MLAs, rushed to the chair of the speaker. Other BSP and SP members also joined them. The sight was extraordinarily horrific as files, chairs and even microphones were uprooted and flung at the speaker.

Amid this chaos, Kalyan Singh was escorted out by security personnel, but the state assembly had already been converted into a battleground. The house members were now thrashing each other with mikes and chairs, and speaker Keshari Nath Tripathi, shielded by policemen, started reading the governor's message. After almost half an hour of this mayhem, which left several members of the assembly with grave injuries, the confidence motion was discussed and passed 222–0. This was the first time in my journalistic career that I witnessed defections on such an enormous scale taking place during the proceedings of the assembly. Though Kalyan Singh proved his majority in the assembly with the support of rebel MLAs of the Congress and the BSP, the modalities of their split were never clear.

The drama was far from settled even after 21 October 1997. Governor Romesh Bhandari was highly displeased with what had happened in the assembly. He was in favour of President's rule in the state again, but the National Front government at the Centre declined his request. In an attempt to reward all the rebel MLAs, Kalyan Singh created the biggest ever cabinet in India of ninety-four ministers. But things were not normal at all in the politics of UP. Almost four months after Kalyan Singh proved his majority in the house, the political climate of the state once again began to feel the heat of change.

The month was February 1998 and the country was going through polls for the twelfth Lok Sabha. On 21 February 1998, Mayawati held a dramatic press conference in Lucknow where she said she was going to take on the Kalyan Singh government in the state. Around 2 p.m., she reached Raj Bhavan with her BSP MLAs. MLAs from Ajit Singh's Bharaitya Kisan Kamgar Party, the Janata Dal and the Loktantrik Congress also accompanied her. At Raj Bhavan, she declared Jagdambika Pal, transport minister in the Kalyan Singh government, as the leader of the MLAs and asked Romesh Bhandari to suspend the Kalyan Singh-led BJP government. Kalyan Singh, who was then campaigning in Gorakhpur for his party, returned to Lucknow immediately.

This time, Governor Romesh Bhandari was not willing to give him a chance to prove his majority in the assembly. In another uniquely dramatic development in the politics of the state, he suspended the Kalyan Singh government and went on to swear in Jagdambika Pal as CM. This happened around 10 p.m. on 21 February, only eight hours after Mayawati's march to Raj Bhavan. With Pal, Naresh Agrawal was sworn in as deputy CM.

Lucknow was witness to some extraordinary sights the next day. The city was going to the polls, but at the state guest house Vajpayee decided to sit on a fast against what he termed as the arbitrary and one-sided action of Governor Bhandari in dismissing the Kalyan Singh government. The scenes at the Lucknow secretariat were equally dramatic. This was one of the rarest moments in the politics of the state—two leaders were claiming to be its chief minister. Realizing that the situation was tricky, the BJP decided to challenge the constitutionality of Bhandari's decision in the Allahabad High Court.

On 22 February, BJP leader Narendra Singh Gaud filed a petition in the court, and on the very next day the high court ordered restoration of the Kalyan Singh-led BJP government in the state. This was a rude shock to Bhandari and to the Jagdambika Pal camp, who then challenged the high court's decision in the Supreme Court. By then, however, all the rebel MLAs of the Loktantrik Congress had returned to the Kalyan Singh camp and Jagdambika Pal was left in the Lucknow secretariat with the dubious distinction of having been CM for just forty-eight hours.

Undoubtedly, the 1990s in UP saw the peak of switcher activity. Overnight, sometimes, the switchers could make a windfall with their moves. But the switcher trend has not gone away; it endures to date. A section of politicians chooses a political party purely on the basis of its power arrangements with it. In such cases, ideologies don't even find a place in public debates. Often, caste backing is enough reason for the switchers to hold their core vote and also find place for themselves in whichever political party gives them the best power deal.

10

The Agrarian Crisis

Agriculture has been the mainstay for the vast population of India through the ages. In the post-Independence years, it was the sector of agriculture that supplied raw materials for manufacturing and paved the way for India's growth in what looked like a highly destabilizing economic climate during the post-war period. Clearly, those were the times when it enjoyed a dominant position in the economy and was thus cared for, not just rhetorically but substantially, by policymakers and governments in the Centre and states. But then it started sliding into crises and farmer indebtedness. Falling productivity, frequent crop failure and farmer suicides became the hallmark of the Indian agricultural sector. What has characterized this decline is the slump in the agricultural sector in those states that were once flagbearers of the Green Revolution and which had enough fertile land to spearhead their development. UP is one such state.

With almost 59 per cent of its workforce engaged in agricultural activities for their livelihood and 30 per cent of the population living below the poverty line, the state currently presents one of the darkest pictures of the country's agrarian crisis. The numbers speak volumes about the crisis the most populous state of the country is going through. The share of agriculture in UP's gross domestic product has been consistently declining down the years. The growth of the sector in the period 2001–15 averaged 2.5 per cent per annum, below the all-India average of 2.9 per cent during the same period. There are more than 18 million agricultural households in the state, but their average monthly income is the third lowest in the country. The state accounts for the largest share—16.9 per cent—of all indebted agricultural households in India. What makes these numbers more glaring is the fact that almost 90 per cent of the indebted agricultural households in UP are those of marginal and small farmers.

These numbers, in many ways, in themselves convey a broad picture of the crisis the farm sector in the state is facing. But the plight of UP's agriculture sector can't simply be unpacked through these numbers. There is always a larger context to them. One should, therefore, always take into account how the pace of industrialization in states like UP has not picked up post the reforms of the 1990s and how this has left the state heavily banking on the agriculture sector for its economic growth. This is something peculiar to the northern states of the country, including UP, that they rely so much on the health of the farm sector that even a small fluctuation in its fortunes can impact their overall growth index hugely. Seen in this context, the numbers of UP's deteriorating agriculture sector are far more worrying than they appear on paper.

But the agrarian crisis UP is witnessing has many facets, something which has been examined and contextualized at length in a number of studies. There is broad consensus that the Green Revolution of the 1960s benefited the farmers of north Indian states, including UP and Punjab. It was due to these reforms that western UP became known as a sugarcane belt, giving rise to a relatively prosperous and affluent farm class, which farmer–leader Chaudhary Charan Singh represented in the 1960s and '70s. Though it has also been highlighted—and rightly so—that the Green Revolution created pockets of rich farmers across the state and that its benefits were not passed on to small and landless farmers, UP's overall agriculture scenario remained satisfactory.

The recent plight of UP's farm sector really started in the 1990s. These were the years when farmers across the country were exposed to global markets, and each lot was impacted differently. Thus, the highly developed southern states, which mostly grew commercial corps such as cotton, coconut, coffee and onion, became vulnerable to the ups and downs of the global economy. This left a large number of poor cotton farmers in huge financial distress. Coupled with frequent droughts and deficient rains, their financial distress resulted in many of them taking their own lives. The cotton-growing Vidarbha region of Maharashtra became a hotspot of farmer suicides.

The situation in UP too worsened in the post-reform years, but somewhat differently from other states. A section of farmers in the state had already tasted the fruits of the Green Revolution and therefore were positioned better to cash in on the benefits of the 1990s reforms. Still, the sector slumped considerably in the state as poor implementation of government policies and ecological problems suppressed the prospects of agriculture in a big way. It is noteworthy in this regard that UP was witnessing frequent shifts in power during the 1990s, with the result that no welfare scheme or policy could be implemented effectively for long. At times, the leaders heading the state failed to introduce modern technologies among the farmers, so returns from agricultural activity remained very poor for them. This was one of the major reasons why farmers in many different pockets of UP remained deprived of the gains of reforms, which their counterparts in other states were getting.

A comparison of UP with other states along a variety of indicators makes a point in this case. A study on the agriculture crisis in UP conducted by Prof. Rakesh Raman of Banaras Hindu University compared the annual growth rate in the yield of major crops in the major Indian states in 2014. UP ranked seventh in this respect among fourteen Indian states which predominantly relied on agriculture for their economic growth. In the same study, it was demonstrated that the high growth in the population of the state had caused per capita food grain availability to decline in UP. Although, with per capita food grain availability at 234.56 kg in 2012-13, the state ranked a fair third after Punjab (996.74 kg) and Haryana (635.20 kg) and way above the neighbouring states of Madhya Pradesh (201.28 kg) and Bihar (107.2 kg), the fall in these figures since 1990-91 has been a worrisome trend. Many studies have been warning for quite some time now against the declining growth rate of food grain production in the state. While before the 1990s this rate was higher than the population growth rate, the trend has reversed since.

But there is a lot of variability in UP within its own territory when it comes to agricultural performance. The agricultural backwardness of the Bundelkhand region is largely due to its tough climatic conditions, while in the eastern part of UP there has been little technological intervention over the years. But crop failure, stagnant prices and absence of a price support system are equally responsible for the deteriorating condition of farmers in these regions, not to mention faulty procurement operations. Quite often, in several of the state *mandis*, the market prices of wheat and paddy rule 10 per cent to 25 per cent below the minimum support price (MSP). Similar problems face the dairy sector, where the farmers fetch 15–20 per cent lower prices from the cooperative sector than from the private sector. Overall, the prices they get are 15 per cent less than the prices fetched by milk farmers in Gujarat. Sugarcane, another prominent crop in UP, has suffered as it has been in the clutches of distortionary pricing policies. In addition to lack of proper price incentives, lack of adequate infrastructure—rural road connectivity, rural power, cold storages, warehouses—has impeded agricultural growth in UP.

One astonishing aspect of Indian politics is that it has failed to alleviate the distress of Indian farmers even though no political party or politician has ever dared to get on the wrong side of the farmers, they being the biggest vote bank. Over 60 per cent of India's workforce still toils in its agricultural fields. Yet, their fortunes have never changed holistically, despite the many government schemes, promises, recommendations and committees that have been constituted over the years, ostensibly to solve farmer distress. This is one of the starkest realities of Indian governance, and UP has been no different. In fact, the farmer protest of 2020-21 only demonstrates that Indian farmers still feel that they are not being given their due by governments.

In my years of rural reporting and travel across villages in India, in particular UP, the deep-rooted question one is led to ultimately ask is: does the benefit of government schemes reach those who need it most? The answer is: not always. I got the most startling picture of this during my travels across UP in April 2015. For the first time as a reporter, I saw first-hand and understood the devastating impact of unseasonal rains on farmers. The crops were simply destroyed, and the farmers got no immediate help to manage their distress and their urgent need for money. This is the pain and plight of landless farmers in India.

After travelling across UP, starting from Noida and ending my journey in the Chambal region, I wrote a column 'Who will dry Radha's tears?' This was the story of Radha reported by me on NDTV from a small village in Mathura. This story was aired on 22 April 2015. Radha's story contained in it the whole story of 'Landless India'. Much of the farm labour that tills the soil for us doesn't exist in the eyes of the government as it never finds its way into government records and never gets to benefit from the big government schemes. The star MP from Mathura, Hema Malini, was once heckled by locals during a rally by the prime minister for her apathy towards the plight of contract farm labourers in her constituency.

A telling event that uncovered this deep-rooted crisis in UP for all to see was the flight of poor labourers from across the country on foot to make it back to their villages in UP during the coronavirus pandemic. This happened after the announcement of a hasty national lockdown in March 2020. The disturbing and horrifying images of poor labourers covering thousands of kilometres on foot to reach their homes in their villages in UP astounded the nation. The real reason for their leaving their home state in the first place was to look for work in other states, of course. Most of them were landless farm labourers. In 2016, I had written in one of my columns—much before we knew that the world would face a pandemic—that their state is so fragile that they can no longer depend on agriculture for their livelihood. Going by National Sample Survey Organization (NSSO) data, the number of the effectively landless has increased considerably over the decades, leaving them with no option but to work for landowners for a living. And any disturbance in the ecosystem—like unseasonal rains, market price fluctuations, corruption in the local *mandis*—makes survival very difficult for them. They are then forced to make it to the big cities to look for work. Mumbai, as I have known and witnessed for years, has been flooded with armies of displaced immigrant farmers from UP who do odd jobs and can even be seen begging and scrounging for a living on the streets. It was many of these that we saw walking across the country back to their homes when the corona crisis happened.

With the painful story of UP now flashed across the country in newspapers and on television, the state government ordered an exercise of skill-mapping so that these labourers could find work in their own state. This should have been done by the governments of the state decades ago. It would have stopped the mass exodus of poor farm labourers in search of work to other states.

The plight and poverty of these landless farmers are also the result of the financial trap they get into. It starts with their borrowing money from the local money lords or *sahookar* to do farming on someone else's land on a contractual basis, referred to as *adhiya* in the local UP dialect. And from here starts the vicious cycle for the local landless farmer. He is indebted to the moneylender, and if the crop fails, he has to repay the moneylender and at times the landowner too, who too he may have borrowed money from. Inability to repay these people brings him so much stress that he often dies from it or commits suicide. An even worse reality is the absence of compensation for the family of a person who commits suicide out of economic compulsions. With the bread winner gone, there is now no one to support his family. This was the story of Radha and her little children in UP.

In UP, the hotbed of farmer politics, protests and agitations has been its western region adjoining Delhi. The farmers from the region have led major protests against governments in Delhi and have been more vocal than their counterparts in eastern UP, Purvanchal or even Bundelkhand. One can recall how in the 1980s, farm movements led by the Bharatiya Kisan Union (BKU) leader Mahendra Singh Tikait against high power tariffs and poor power supply shook the politics of UP. In 1988, Tikait appealed to the peasants in Meerut to take up their own cause and organized lakhs of them to demonstrate. But the farmers of western UP are on the whole less poor and are mostly in ownership of land, even if only small patches, whereas the farm labourers working for landowners in eastern UP are very poor and helpless. Eastern UP is also the most populous as well as the poorest region of UP.

The relative affluence of the farmers of western UP is also attributed to the crop they farm—sugarcane. The region hosts several sugar mills too. Over the years, sugarcane farming has brought rich dividends to farmers in this part of the state. This has resulted in their abandonment of conventional crops, such as wheat and paddy, as they no longer depend on them. Though delayed payments on the part of mill owners in the region have hit the headlines in the recent past, the situation of farmers in western UP has remained much better than that of their counterparts in the rest of the state.

This is precisely why they were dominating the months-long farm protests that went on in the national capital. There is a prevalent perception among them that the Modi government's agriculture legislation will deprive them of their most prized possession—land. They perceive the recommendation of contract farming in the new legislation as a threat to their survival. And this time too, the man at the centrestage of the farm protest was another Tikait from the region—the son of Mahendra Singh Tikait, Rakesh Singh Tikait. The persistent protest finally forced the government to buckle and withdraw its controversial laws by the end of 2021.

Conclusion

Having examined all the facets of Uttar Pradesh that have a bearing on its politics—its deep-rooted social reality of caste and its role in the state's politics, the collapse of the Congress in the state, the political bastions in the state, the extraordinary criminality and communalization that beset its politics, and its agrarian crisis—it is imperative to ask where does UP go from here. What are the possible challenges that it needs to overcome in the near future to live up to the expectations of its huge population?

In this concluding chapter of the book, I try to paint a broad picture of the state, describing where it has improved and what it needs to work upon for a better future.

Any discussion on Uttar Pradesh has to start with its complex demography, a distinction that always made it stand out in India. It is home to almost one-sixth of India's population and has remarkably diverse regional cultures. It has been rightly called a 'country' and not a state. In terms of its population, it has been from time to time compared with the UK, France, Germany, and of course with our neighbour, Pakistan, as it surpassed these countries in population over the years. Geographically, it is a huge state nestled in the northern part of India. It is land-locked, with no direct access to the sea—considered a natural disadvantage for the state and also one of the reasons for its weak growth pattern over the years. In many ways, the compulsion to keep looking at UP along these lines has not changed with successive governments and policymakers.

Without any doubt, its large population and the high population growth rate are the biggest challenges for the state. To put it in perspective, a patch of land slightly over 7 per cent of the total area of the country houses almost 15 per cent of its total population. Handling such a large number of people—and a dense population at that—of many different and distinct communities, castes and groups has always been a daunting task for governments. The decadal population growth in UP is higher than the national average, a trend that is worrisome, but in recent years, with a significant decline in the total fertility rate, the population growth in the state is slowing slightly. It has been demonstrated consistently in the past few years' economic surveys of the country that UP has reached the next phase of demographic transition, from where its population growth will slow down in the next two decades.

The key solution for UP would be to take advantage of this demographic transition, and this would naturally depend on the future governments and their policymakers' ability to give momentum to this demographic decline. UP has not been able to achieve a decline in population since the 1970s. It was from this decade that the state appeared an anomaly compared with the rest of the country. From the 1970s to the 2000s, the national-level population growth declined, but not in the case of UP, making it difficult for the state to compete with other states. (Of course, now a population control law is being proposed by the state government and is a hotly debated development).

In order to make the most of its demographic shift southward, the future governments of UP should identify the key areas of concern and put in place policies that address them positively and in a time-bound manner. It's very important to understand that the benefits of demographic shifts do not come naturally; you need to have proper policies and programmes in place.

From this perspective, the biggest challenge is public health. Health should always be a key area of concern; investment in public health is investment in human resources. But with the Covid-19 pandemic, public health has suddenly emerged as one of the top priorities for any government anywhere in the world. The belief now is that handling of public health would be a key determinant of any country's overall performance and development in the near future. This seems absolutely true, given the threat the coronavirus pandemic has posed to every country's health system, irrespective of the country's social and economic standing. And the pandemic has not been an ordinary threat. It has been an existential crisis for humanity, demonstrating that investment in health cannot be compromised. The task ahead for the most populous state of the country is going to be far more difficult and challenging than for any other in this regard.

The pandemic has clearly demonstrated that the state has to pump a lot of capital into its basic medical infrastructure, especially in rural areas, where the majority of its population lives. Without drastically improving primary healthcare services in the interiors of the state, the pathetic state of UP's health system is unlikely to change. This involves a number of tasks, from building adequate physical infrastructure to creating a huge medical workforce that can cover the entire rural region of the state. On both fronts, the state currently presents a very dark picture. There are only 18,000 sanctioned posts for doctors in government hospitals in UP. This figure in itself is indicative of the huge crisis the state faces, as, given its population of almost 20 crore, this works out to one doctor for 10,000 people. Since the majority of the people living in the rural parts of the state can't afford the expensive services of private hospitals, they mostly rely on government hospitals. So, the acute shortage of staff in public hospitals is very alarming.

The problem of quality physical infrastructure, in the form of hospitals, is also something that has come under severe criticism in UP, but in my view that is the secondary issue. The focus should be on staffing hospitals with doctors, nurses and technicians, and in ensuring the availability and maintenance of equipment and supply of drugs. If this alone is achieved, it would mean a huge health turnaround for the state. It is crucial to note that most of the efforts aimed at improvement of the state's poor health services fail because there is hardly any change at the grassroots level. It has been widely reported over the years that most of UP's community healthcare centres located in the remote villages do have some physical infrastructure but no workforce to make them operational.

It was this gap more than anything else that the coronavirus pandemic, with all its consequences, brought to the fore. The handling of the pandemic became challenging for the state government precisely because of the limited human resources at its disposal. One should also not forget that the public's perception of the coronavirus disease, especially in the rural areas of the state, also contributed significantly to the worsening of the situation. This is also a typically UP phenomenon, arising from the low levels of education and awareness in the state, particularly in the highly populated region of eastern UP. This made it difficult for the authorities to execute their disease-control strategies. The unimaginable scale of reverse migration of workers from different parts of the country to their villages also put a huge burden on state resources during the pandemic.

Thus, enduring reforms in the health sector are something that successive governments in the state should target. In this effort, they should coordinate with the Centre and make sure the budget allocated for health is utilized to the maximum and brings improvement at the ground level in the state. It goes without saying that the Centre should also reprioritize its healthcare spend, and the signs in this direction are already positive. In 2020-21, India allocated only 1.8 per cent of its GDP to healthcare. But with health and well-being becoming one of the six pillars of the Union Budget 2021-22, the government committed 2.5–3 per cent of GDP for healthcare.

UP could also learn from the healthcare models of other states that have done well in delivering healthcare services to their people. Many of the southern states have utilized private investments in the health sector to their advantage by opening medical colleges. This has not yet happened in UP very effectively. A public–private approach can perhaps do wonders for public healthcare in UP if implemented in the right spirit.

UP also needs to be socio-economically inclusive. Currently, its average per capita income is around half of India's, but at the time of Independence the state's per capita income wasn't so dismal and stood somewhat on a par with the rest of India's. To maintain this, it required to accelerate growth, but its measures did not keep pace with the population growth in the decades between the 1970s and 2000s. There were some patchy periods of good performance, for example, in the decade of 1980–1990, when its growth rate really picked up, but the state completely failed to capitalize on it.

The key reason for this was, of course, the politics of the 1990s, characterized by casteism and communalism, which dealt a decisive blow to UP's growth. While the economic reforms of 1990 brought in a new era in India where every state planned its developmental strategy from a fresh perspective, keeping in mind the new set of economic and social challenges that were emerging, the states of the Hindi heartland were notoriously trapped in the age-old issues of caste and religion. No government during this period was able to come up with plans or schemes that could put UP at the top, or at least in the race in the competitive world of post-reforms India.

While the rest of India grew at an average rate of 6.8 per cent per annum between 1990 and 2004, UP completely veered off the growth path. In fact, in the pre-liberalization period, the gap between the country's per capita income growth rate and that of UP had been less than 1 percentage point, but this widened to over 3 percentage points in the post-reforms period. UP managed to compensate for this loss to some extent after 2005, but could not fully bridge the growth-rate gap with the rest of the country, which remained fluctuating between 1 and 2 percentage points. It is this glaring gap that successive governments should plan to address, and that's where the potential of demographic transition that I have talked about earlier is significant.

Another social indicator that requires attention when we talk about UP and overhaul of its growth pattern is employment. The problem of unemployment has always plagued the state, and of course it is connected to the state's high population. The question of how to employ the young and productive component of the state's population has always remained a challenge for policymakers. Not long ago, there were discussions on how its predominantly young population gives UP an edge over other states. It's true that a third of UP's population consists of youth and this holds enormous potential for the future growth of the state. But that is where the challenge lies too. The mere availability of a young workforce will not automatically translate into growth for the state. The workforce needs to be made employable and labour-intensive industries must come up to absorb them. The creation of such industries will be vital for the realization of the potential of this workforce.

Where does UP stand now, from the perspective of all these factors? The answer is not very encouraging but not very discouraging either.

The images of migrant labourers walking back to UP during the coronavirus pandemic will haunt the nation for years to come. In light of this, the UP government's announcement of conducting a skill-mapping exercise should have been done by the earlier governments decades ago, as I have said earlier. And through this skill mapping, coupled with relevant vocational training of young men and women, the state can transform its workforce into a unique powerhouse. UP's young men and women will not have to leave their homeland in such large numbers in search of work in other states. It's not that the state has not gone through the process of industrialization; it has achieved handsomely in this regard, but the problem has been one of unsustainability.

First of all, as a sign of encouragement, the unemployment rate in UP has been on a continual decline. Much to the relief of its workforce and the government, it was recorded at 6.9 per cent in June 2021, against 21 per cent last year, when the state was going through pandemic-induced lockdowns. Even in the pre-pandemic period, the state was right on track in creating a skilled workforce through the promotion of medium and small industries. The current state government has rightly recognized the importance of skill development programmes. By infusing funds into them at regular intervals, it has made sure that the programmes did not derail completely even during the pandemic.

In spirit and intention, these efforts are well placed. The only issue is to ensure their success in the long run, without which the broad picture of unemployment in the state cannot change. It is not surprising that UP always struggles to achieve consistency in its rate of unemployment, which fluctuates widely, reflecting the inefficacy of the policies and programmes in place in creating consistent change. That is because steadiness in skill development also depends on the kind of education we provide in our schools, colleges and institutes of higher education. In order to make education skill-oriented, the need of the hour is to rethink our education policies and curricula and rearticulate and realign them to make them compatible with the broader scenario of employment in the state. The sector of primary education is also one that requires improvement. Currently, higher educational institutes in the state do not generate employable graduates, a fact that adds to the dismal record of unemployment in the state. On all these fronts, a complete overhaul of the conventional policies would be required. By largely containing the working population of UP in UP itself, its growth story can be changed completely in the decades to come.

UP has relied for growth on its agricultural sector for far too long. But this cannot continue as its population grows. For sure, in order to meet the demands of its rising population, it has to raise farm productivity. This is especially true of the eastern part of UP, where yields of rice and wheat do not come close to those of Punjab and Haryana. Relatively prosperous western UP has managed to produce commercial crops like sugarcane and potato, but the eastern and central parts of the state have not been able to achieve this. These are some potential opportunities for improvement as far as the agriculture sector of the state is concerned.

But growth in the agriculture sector in UP relies excessively on rains and this is a limitation. For the state to accelerate growth, it's crucial to focus on industrial development and the infrastructure that this would entail. The biggest transformation for the state in the last couple of decades has been the creation of excellent road networks, which has smoothened industrial movement in the state to a great extent. UP's expressways are the new hallmark of its development. While the Yamuna Expressway connecting Delhi and Agra came up in 2012 and the Agra–Lucknow Expressway was opened to the public in 2018, many more such projects are lined up for the future—the 340-kilometre Purvanchal, the 296-kilometre Bundelkhand, the 91-kilometre Gorakhpur and the 594-kilometre Ganga expressways, to name just a few. It is estimated that on the completion of these projects, the total network of expressways would add up to 1,788 kilometres, the highest in the country.

With such an extensive and ambitious road network, the state is all set to improve its poor record of industrial development. But here too, there are challenges. Though, in recent times, the state has markedly improved its rank in ease of doing business (it has been rated as the second best in the country), the perception that this state does not provide a conducive environment for doing business persists. There is increasing demand that the state should work on its tax structure to simplify it. There are similar demands for the simplification of the tariff structure for electricity too. Power should be priced moderately to attract investors, it is often argued and demanded.

One area pertaining to industrial development is exports; export industries have the huge potential to create jobs within the territory of the state. They are an opportunity for future governments of the state to invest in, to improve the rate of employment.

It is impossible to overlook the services sector—transport, hotels, financial services, public services, real estate. This is again an expanding sector and presents an excellent opportunity for policymakers to accelerate domestic growth.

In the context of UP's complex demography, its size makes its administrative handling a challenge in itself. Of course, this has led to a section of the political class demanding division of the state into four. There is no denying that the large administrative area of UP makes governance a tough challenge. This difficulty is further exacerbated by the fact that all of its major regions—western UP, eastern UP, central UP and Bundelkhand—are geographically uneven in terms of the number of districts in each. While western and eastern UP have nearly thirty, central UP and Bundelkhand have just about one-third of that figure or less.

Given the diverse nature and culture of these regions, policy must deal with them separately. A uniform central policy for all these regions will simply not work. The budgetary allocations made to these regions have also not been effective precisely for this reason, and the story of the Bundelkhand package discussed earlier illustrates the deep-rooted problem of corruption which has distorted the distribution of funds. Still, the demand to divide UP into four states has led to a huge uproar on many an occasion.

So, in conclusion, the future of UP really depends on the consistency and steadiness with which it pursues socio-economic development. The past shows it has done well in patches, so progress is possible, the real challenge being to make it consistent. This would depend on many factors. It is hoped that the future governments of the state will not allow it to slump again. UP is a state of skilled people, and to press them into employment for the state itself will ensure the people and the state a better future.

Notes

1. Subhash Mishra, 'Samajwadi Party leader Mulayam Singh Yadav tries to shed pro-Muslim image,' *India Today*, 5 February 2007, https://www.indiatoday.in/magazine/indiascope/story/20070205-mulayam-trying-to-get-rid-of-image-of-pro-muslim-748992-2007-02-05.
2. Tariq Thachil, 'Elite Parties and Poor Voters: Theory and Evidence from India,' *The American Political Science Review*, Vol. 108, No. 2 (2014): 454–77. http://www.jstor.org/stable/43654383.
3. Sunita Aron, *Ballots and Breakups: The Games Politicians Play* (New Delhi: Bloomsbury India, 2019).
4. Rekha Datta, 'Hindu Nationalism or Pragmatic Party Politics? A Study of India's Hindu Party,' *International Journal of Politics,*

Culture, and Society, Vol. 12, No. 4 (1999): 573–88. http://www.jstor.org/stable/20019991.

5. Christophe Jaffrelot, *The Hindu Nationalist Movement and Indian Politics: 1925 to the 1990s* (London: C Hurst & Co Publishers Ltd., 1996), 225.
6. *NDTV India*, 19 April 2019, https://ndtv.in/lok-sabha-elections-2019/what-is-guest-house-kand-which-crates-gulf-between-mayawati-and-mulayam-singh-yadav-2025596.
7. Sydney H. Schanberg, 'Mrs. Gandhi Ousts State Government,' *The New York Times*, 3 October 1970, https://www.nytimes.com/1970/10/03/archives/mrs-gandhi-ousts-state-government.html.
8. Jyoti Yadav, 'Brahmin pride and pain flood Facebook after Vikas Dubey's encounter killing,' *The Print*, 10 July 2020, https://theprint.in/opinion/pov/brahmin-pride-pain-flood-facebook-vikas-dubey-encounter-killing/458417/.
9. Subhash Mishra, 'Increase in crime, mafia activity puts Uttar Pradesh CM Kalyan Singh on the defensive,' *India Today*, 6 July 1998, https://www.indiatoday.in/magazine/states/story/19980706-increase-in-crime-mafia-activity-puts-uttar-pradesh-cm-kalyan-singh-on-the-defensive-826566-1998-07-06.
10. Manoj Singh, 'Vikas Dubey Is the Symptom of a Political System That Provides Patronage to Criminals,' *The Wire*, 9 July 2020, https://thewire.in/politics/vikas-dubey-politics-criminals-nexus-uttar-pradesh-bihar.
11. Rajeev Dikshit and Pathikrit Chakraborty, 'Man who introduced Kalashnikov to UP gang wars,' *The Times of India*, 10 July 2018, http://timesofindia.indiatimes.com/articleshow/64925169.

cms?utm_source=contentofinterest&utm_medium=text&utm_campaign=cppst.

12. 'Profile: India's dreaded gangster,' *BBC News*, 11 November 2005, http://news.bbc.co.uk/2/hi/south_asia/4427536.stm.
13. 'What is Behmai massacre case', *The Times of India*, 6 January 2020, http://timesofindia.indiatimes.com/articleshow/73115160.cms?utm_source=contentofinterest&utm_medium=text&utm_campaign=cppst https://timesofindia.indiatimes.com/india/what-is-behmai-massacre-case/articleshow/73115160.cms.
14. 'Kurmi' is a backward caste whose members are predominantly from UP and Bihar.

    Deepak Gidwani, 'After Dadua, Thokia calls the shots in UP ravines,' *DNA*, 19 November 2013, https://www.dnaindia.com/india/report-after-dadua-thokia-calls-the-shots-in-up-ravines-1111866.

    Aakar Patel, 'Caste order: the Patel is the new "shudra",' *Mint*, 8 August 2015, https://www.livemint.com/Leisure/7Cpjv1gvzl7xZKf8M0sU8H/Caste-order-the-Patel-is-the-new-shudra.html.
15. 'Making Money from Tendu Leaves', *The Times of India*, 23 July 2007.
16. It is the conclusion of many journalists and reporters who followed these events closely at the time that the Rajiv Gandhi government persuaded the court to make that order.

    Hemant Sharma, *Ayodhya: A Battleground* (New Delhi: Rupa Publications, 2020), 240, where he writes: 'An appeal was filed at the Faizabad court on 31 January 1986 for unlocking the birthplace. Vir Bahadur Singh didn't want the credit to go to the VHP, so Arun Nehru and Vir Bahadur Singh advised Rajiv Gandhi to open the disputed premises and the lock was opened immediately, barely forty minutes after the court's verdict.' See also: 'Unlocking of Babri Masjid was a "balancing act" by then government: Arif Mohammed Khan,' *The Indian Express*, 28 March 2017, https://www.newindianexpress.com/nation/2017/mar/28/unlocking-of-babri-masjid-was-a-balancing-act-by-then-government-arif-mohammed-khan-1586887.html.

17. Text of BJP Palampur resolution. See also: Hemant Sharma, *Ayodhya: A Battleground* (New Delhi: Rupa Publications, 2020), 124.
18. Ibid.
19. Based on my conversations with Pramod Mahajan while I was a reporter.
20. Excerpts from Hemant Sharma, *Yuddha Mein Ayodhya* (New Delhi: Prabhat Prakashan, 2018).
21. 'Guest house "assault": The 1995 infamous incident that had turned SP-BSP bitter foes,' *The Indian* Express, 14 January 2019, https://indianexpress.com/article/what-is/the-1995-infamous-guest-house-incident-that-had-turned-sp-bsp-bitter-foes-5537680/.

    Ravish Tiwari, 'The story of the Guest House,' *The Indian Express*, 16 January 2019, https://indianexpress.com/article/explained/mayawati-akhilesh-yadav-sp-bsp-alliance-guest-house-attack-5540258/.

References

1: The Political Change Agenda

Sunita Aron, *Ballots and Breakups: The Games Politicians Play* (New Delhi: Bloomsbury India, 2019).

Books and Journals

Roger Jeffery, Craig Jeffrey and Jens Lerche, eds. *Development Failure and Identity Politics in Uttar Pradesh* (New Delhi: Sage Publications India Pvt Ltd, 2014), http://dx.doi.org/10.4135/9789351507895.

Paul Brass, Introduction in 'The Politics of India since Independence,' *The New Cambridge History of India,* (Cambridge: Cambridge University Press, 1994).

Paul Brass, 'The Politicization of the Peasantry in a North Indian state—Part 2,' *The Journal of Peasant Studies*, 1980, 8(1), 3–36.

Paul Brass, 'Chaudhary Charan Singh: An Indian Political Life,' *Economic and Political Weekly*, 1993, 28 (39), 2087–2090.

New Farmers' Movements in India, ed. Tom Brass (Ilford: Franck, 1995).

Bidyut Chakrabarty, *Indian Politics and Society since Independence: Events, Processes and Ideology*, 1st ed., 2008.

Christophe Jaffrelot, *India's Silent Revolution: The Rise of the Lower Castes in North India* (New York: Columbia University Press, 2003).

Christophe Jaffrelot, *Dr Ambedkar and Untouchability: Analysing and Fighting Caste* (New Delhi: Permanent Black, 2004).

Christophe Jaffrelot, *The Hindu Nationalist Movement and Indian Politics—1925 to 1990s* (New York: Columbia University Press, 1996). Suhas Palshikar, 'Beyond Uttar Pradesh: New Implications for Party Politics,' *Economic and Political Weekly*, 2007, 42(21), 1890–1892.

Zoya Hasan, *Quest for Power: Oppositional Movements and Post-Congress Politics in Uttar Pradesh* (New Delhi: Oxford University Press, 1998).

Pradyot Lal & Tara Nair, *Caste vs Caste: Turbulence in Indian Politics* (New Delhi: Ajanta, 1998).

K. K. Verma, *Changing Role of Caste Associations* (New Delhi: National Publishing House, 1979).

Charan Singh, *Joint Farming X-Rayed: The Problem and Its Solution* (Bombay: Bharatiya Vidya Bhavan, 1959).

Charan Singh, *India's Poverty and Its Solution* (New York: Asia Publishing House, 1964).

Charan Singh, *Land Reforms in UP and the Kulaks* (New Delhi: Vikas, 1986).

Arun Shourie, *Worshipping False Gods: Ambedkar, and the Facts Which Have Been Erased* (New Delhi: ASA Publications, 1986).

Sekhar Bandyopadhyay, 'Transfer of Power and the Crisis of Dalit Politics in India, 1945–47,' *Modern Asian Studies*, 2000, 34/4: 913.

Rammanohar Lohia, *The Caste System* (Hyderabad: Rammanohar Lohia Samata Vidyalaya, 1979).

2: The Caste Crunch

Books and Journals

Paul Brass, Introduction in 'The Politics of India since Independence,' *The New Cambridge History of India*, (Cambridge: Cambridge University Press, 1994).

Paul Brass, 'The Politicization of the Peasantry in a North Indian state – Part 2,' *The Journal of Peasant Studies*, 1980, 8(1), 3–36.

Paul Brass, 'Factionalism and the Congress Party in Uttar Pradesh,' *Asian Survey*, 1964, 4(9), 1037–1047.

Paul Brass, 'Chaudhary Charan Singh: An Indian Political Life,' *Economic and Political Weekly*, 1993, 28(39), 2087–2090.

New Farmers' Movements in India, ed. Tom Brass (Ilford: Franck, 1995).

Bidyut Chakrabarty, *Indian Politics and Society since Independence: Events, Processes and Ideology*, 1st ed., 2008.

Christophe Jaffrelot, *India's Silent Revolution: The Rise of the Lower Castes in North India* (New York: Columbia University Press, 2003).

Christophe Jaffrelot, *Dr Ambedkar and Untouchability: Analysing and Fighting Caste* (New Delhi: Permanent Black, 2004).

Christophe Jaffrelot, *The Hindu Nationalist Movement and Indian Politics—1925 to 1990s* (New York: Columbia University Press, 1996).

Sudha Pai and Sajjan Kumar, *Everyday Communalism: Riots in Contemporary Uttar Pradesh* (New Delhi: Oxford University Press, 2018).

Christophe Jaffrelot and K. Sanjay, *The Marginalization of the Savarnas in Uttar Pradesh* (New Delhi: Routledge, 2009).

Ian Duncan, 'Agricultural Innovation and Political Change in North India,' *The Journal of Peasant Studies,* 1997, 24(4): 246–6.

Ian Duncan, 'New Political Equations in North India—Mayawati, Mulayam and Government Instability in Uttar Pradesh,' *Asian Survey,* 1997.

Government of India, *Report of the Backward Classes Commission*, N. d. 1955, Vol. 1. Delhi.

Government of India, *Report of the Backward Classes Commission*, First Part, N. d. 1980, Vols. 1 and 2, New Delhi.

Government of India, *Constituent Assembly Debates*, N. d, Lok Sabha Secretariat. 1989, Vols. 1 and 2, New Delhi.

Zoya Hasan, *Quest for Power: Oppositional Movements and Post-Congress Politics in Uttar Pradesh* (New Delhi: Oxford University Press, 1998).

Pradyot Lal and Tara Nair, *Caste vs Caste: Turbulence in Indian Politics* (New Delhi: Ajanta Publications, 1998).

K. K. Verma, *Changing Role of Caste Associations* (New Delhi: National Publishing House, 1979).

Charan Singh, *Joint Farming X-Rayed: The Problem and Its Solution* (Bombay: Bharatiya Vidya Bhavan, 1979).

Charan Singh, *India's Poverty and Its Solution* (New York: Asia Publishing House, 1964).

Charan Singh, *Land Reforms in UP and the Kulaks* (New Delhi: Vikas, 1964).

Arun Shourie, *Worshipping False Gods: Ambedkar, and the Facts Which Have Been Erased* (New Delhi: ASA Publications, 1997).

Sekhar Bandyopadhyay, 'Transfer of Power and the Crisis of Dalit Politics in India, 1945–47,' *Modern Asian Studies,* 2000, 34(4): 913.

Rammanohar Lohia, *The Caste System* (Hyderabad: Navahind, 1964).

Ramnarayan S. Rawat, 'Partition Politics and Achhut Identity: A Study of the Scheduled Castes Federation and Dalit Politics in UP, 1946–48,' ed. S. Kaul, *The Partitions of Memory: The Afterlife of the Division of India* (New Delhi: Permanent Black, 2001), 114–15.

Websites

Statistical Reports of general elections to State Assembly (Vidhan Sabha).

Uttar Pradesh, 1951, 1957, 1962, 1967, https://eci.gov.in/statistical-report/statistical-reports/.

1931 Census of India for the United Province of Agra and Avadh, https://dspace.gipe.ac.in/xmlui/handle/10973/18986.

The Times of India, 10 May 1933, 26 November 1954, 2 December 1954, 5 April 1965, 17 August 1967, 18 February 1968, https://search.proquest.com/hnptimesofindia/.

Akshaya Mukul, 'Ram Manohar Lohia: The Quota Marshall,' *The Times of India*, 3 April 2010, https://timesofindia.indiatimes.com/india/ram-manohar-lohia-the-quota-marshall/articleshow/5756713.cms.

Sanya Dhingra, 'Who are Thakurs of UP and why are they powerful? Answers are key to understanding Hathras,' *The Print*, 9 October 2020, https://theprint.in/india/who-are-thakurs-of-up-and-why-are-they-powerful-answers-are-key-to-understanding-hathras/519418/.

Sujay Biswas, 'When Gandhi and Ambedkar came together to settle the Dalit question,' *National Herald*, 20 October 2019, https://www.nationalheraldindia.com/opinion/when-gandhi-and-ambedkar-came-together-to-settle-the-dalit-question.

Sanjoy Chakravorty, 'Viewpoint: How the British reshaped India's caste system,' *BBC News*, 19 June 2019, https://www.bbc.com/news/world-asia-india-48619734.

'Political Demands of Scheduled Castes,' Scheduled Castes Federation, 1944, https://www.constitutionofindia.net/historical_constitutions/political_demands_of_scheduled_castes__scheduled_castes_federation_1944__23rd%20September%201944.

3: The Growth and Growth of Caste

Books and Journals

Christophe Jaffrelot, 'The Rise of the Other Backward Classes in the Hindi Belt,' *The Journal of Asian Studies*, 2000, 59(1), 86–108.

Christophe Jaffrelot, 'Caste and Politics,' *India International Centre Quarterly*, 2000, 37(2), 94–116.

Lewis P. Fickett, 'The Rise and Fall of the Janata Dal,' *Asian Survey*, 1993, 33(12), 1151–1162.

Zoya Hasan, *Congress after Indira: Policy, Power, Political Change (1984-2009)* (New Delhi: Oxford University Press, 2015).

Abdul Gafoor Abdul Majeed Noorani, *The Babri Masjid Question, 1528-2003: A Matter of National Honour,* (New Delhi: Tulika Books, 2003).

Badri Narayan, *Fascinating Hindutva: Saffron Politics and Dalit Mobilization* (New Delhi: Sage Publications Ltd, 2009).

Badri Narayan, *Kanshiram: Leader of the Dalits* (New Delhi: Penguin Random House, 2014).

Dhirendra K. Jha, *Shadow Armies: Fringe Organizations and Foot Soldiers of Hindutva* (New Delhi: Juggernaut Books, 2019).

Hemant Sharma, *Yuddha Mein Ayodhya* (New Delhi: Prabhat Prakashan, 2018).

K. Anshuman, *Yadav Raj: Inside the First Family of Uttar Pradesh* (New Delhi: Penguin Random House, 2017).

Sudha Pai and Sajjan Kumar, *Everyday Communalism: Riots in Contemporary Uttar Pradesh* (New Delhi: Oxford University Press, 2018).

Sudha Pai, Pradeep Sharma, P. Kanungo and R. Mukherji, 'Uttar Pradesh in the 1990s: Critical Perspectives on Society, Polity and Economy,' *Economic and Political Weekly*, 2005, 40(21), 2144–2147.

S. Bayly, 'History and the Fundamentalists: India after the Ayodhya Crisis,' *Bulletin of the American Academy of Arts and Sciences*, 1993, 46(7), 7–26.

Websites

V. Krishna Ananth, 'Why 1967 general election was a watershed in Indian politics and the lessons it left behind,' *DNA*, 28 February 2017, https://www.dnaindia.com/analysis/column-1967-poll-that-changed-india-2330738.

Shyamlal Yadav, 'Uttar Pradesh: A political history', *The Indian Express*, 11 March 2017, https://indianexpress.com/article/explained/uttar-pradesh-assembly-elections-2017-bjp-samajwadi-party-akhilesh-yadav-narendra-modi-rahul-gandhi-mayawati-mulayam-singh-yadav-congress-4562628/.

Dilip Awasthy, 'Uttar Pradesh polls: Dissolution of Assembly sets the stage for another chaotic contest,' *India Today*, 15 November 1995, https://www.indiatoday.in/magazine/cover-story/story/19951115-uttar-pradesh-polls-dissolution-of-assembly-sets-the-stage-for-another-chaotic-electoral-contest-807955-1995-11-15.

Dilip Awasthy, 'Mayawati's installation as first Dalit CM of Uttar Pradesh likely to trigger off realignment of caste equations in all political parties,' *India Today*, 15 November 1995, https://www.indiatoday.in/magazine/cover-story/story/19950630-mayawatis-installation-as-first-dalit-cm-of-uttar-pradesh-likely-to-trigger-off-realignment-of-caste-equations-808382-1995-06-30.

Inderjit Badhwar, 'Office didn't corrupt V.P. Singh, but it showed him up for what he was—not yet a leader,' *India Today*, 15 November 1990, https://www.indiatoday.in/magazine/cover-story/story/19901115-office-didnt-corrupt-v.p.-singh-but-it-showed-him-up-for-what-he-was-not-yet-a-leader-813238-1990-11-15.

Sudha Pai, 'Indian politics has undergone a tremendous change. Uttar Pradesh results the proof,' *The Economic Times*, 26 May 2019, https://economictimes.indiatimes.com/news/elections/lok-sabha/uttar-pradesh/indian-politics-has-undergone-a-tremendous-change-uttar-pradesh-results-the-proof/articleshow/69498432.cms.

Dilip Awasthi, 'Faulty campaign, opposition wave, rout Congress(I) in Uttar Pradesh,' *India Today*, 15 December 1989, https://www.indiatoday.in/magazine/nation/story/19891215-faulty-campaign-opposition-wave-rout-congressi-in-uttar-pradesh-816843-1989-12-15.

Suraj Yengde, 'Dalitality: How Kanshiram's politics took shape as cultural activism, angled its fate,' *The Indian Express*, 20 October

2019, https://indianexpress.com/article/opinion/columns/dalitality-missing-kanshirams-journalism-narendra-modi-bsp-6078049/.

'Book Mulayam for firing on Ayodhya "karsewaks" in 1990: VHP,' *Outlook*, 23 November 2017, https://www.outlookindia.com/newsscroll/book-mulayam-for-firing-on-ayodhya-karsewaks-in-1990-vhp/1194787.

4: Collapse of the Congress

Books and Journals

Paul R. Brass, 'Factionalism and the Congress Party in Uttar Pradesh,' *Asian Survey*, 1993, 4(9), 1037–1047.

Praveen Rai and Sanjay Kumar, 'The Decline of Congress Party in Indian Politics,' *Economic and Political Weekly*, 2017, 52(12).

Christopher Candland, 'Congress Decline and Party Pluralism in India,' *Journal of International Affairs,* 1997, 51(1), 19–35.

Zoya Hasan, 'Does the Congress Have a Future,' *Economic and Political Weekly*, 2017, 52(18).

Bidyut Chakrabarty, *Indian Politics and Society since Independence: Events, Processes and Ideology,* 1st ed. (New Delhi: Routledge, 2008).

Christophe Jaffrelot, *India's Silent Revolution: The Rise of the Lower Castes in North India* (New York: Columbia University Press, 2003).

James L. Sundquist, *The Decline and Resurgence of Congress* (Washington, DC: Brookings Institution, 1981).

Rajni Kothari, 'The Congress "System" in India,' *Asian Survey,* 1964, 4(12), 1161–1173.

Websites

Saubhadra Chatterji, 'How Congress votes have shifted to dominant regional parties,' *Hindustan Times*, 18 February 2020, https://www.hindustantimes.com/india-news/how-cong-votes-have-shifted-to-dominant-regional-parties/story-flv5A88ZNFWs5twWj9knkM.html.

'The decline of Congress and its global peers,' *Mint*, 11 August 2017, https://www.livemint.com/Opinion/mXaXzPBPbGVPZNXKQfopMJ/The-decline-of-Congress-and-its-global-peers.html.

B. Pattabhi Sitaramayya, *History of the Indian National Congress (1885-1935)* (Working Committee of the Congress, 1935), https://www.indianculture.gov.in/history-indian-national-congress-1885-1935.

'Where does the Congress go from here?' *India Today*, 3 August 2020, https://www.indiatoday.in/magazine/cover-story/story/20200803-where-does-the-congress-go-from-here-1704026-2020-07-25.

Zoya Hasan, 'Zoya Hasan writes on why India still needs the Congress and why it lost,' *National Herald*, 2 June 2019, https://www.nationalheraldindia.com/opinion/zoya-hasan-writes-on-why-india-still-needs-the-congress-and-why-it-lost.

Prabhash K. Dutta, 'Election results 2019: Are Hindus shunning Congress?' *India Today*, 27 May 2019, https://www.indiatoday.in/elections/lok-sabha-2019/story/election-results-2019-are-hindus-shunning-congress-1535585-2019-05-27.

Baijayant Panda, 'The decay of the Grand Old Party,' *Hindustan Times*, 30 July 2020, https://www.hindustantimes.com/columns/the-decay-of-the-grand-old-party/story-m90JKBGCyd2gsLw5MZw9fN.html.

Ashok Upadhyay, 'RTI: Who is occupying Lutyens zone bungalow for longest time? Record not tabulated, says govt,' *India Today*, 15 July

2019, https://www.indiatoday.in/india/story/rti-who-is-occupying-lutyens-zone-bungalow-for-longest-time-record-not-tabulated-says-govt-1569496-2019-07-15.

Kaushik Deka, 'What's wrong with the Congress?' *India Today*, 3 August 2020, https://www.indiatoday.in/magazine/cover-story/story/20200803-what-s-wrong-with-the-congress-1704025-2020-07-25.

Siddhartha Talya, 'The decline continues,' *Times Now*, 13 November 2020, https://www.timesnownews.com/columns/article/the-decline-continues/681249.

Anand Mishra, 'Lacking leadership and resources, is Congress in terminal decline?' *Deccan Herald*, 29 November 2020, https://www.deccanherald.com/specials/lacking-leadership-resources-is-congress-in-terminal-decline-921182.html.

T.J.S. George, 'Decline and fall of the Congress. Again,' *The Indian Express*, 20 December 2020, https://www.newindianexpress.com/opinions/columns/t-j-s-george/2020/dec/20/decline--fall-of-the-congress-again-2238511.html.

Ruhi Tewari, 'Not Yogi, but failure of Mayawati, Akhilesh, Rahul is UP's big political story since 2017,' *The Print*, 10 February 2021, https://theprint.in/opinion/politricks/not-yogi-but-failure-of-mayawati-akhilesh-rahul-is-ups-big-political-story-since-2017/602063/.

Sobhana K. Nair, 'Analysis: Priyanka Gandhi moots Congress going solo in Uttar Pradesh in 2022,' *The Hindu*, 30 October 2019, https://www.thehindu.com/news/national/news-analysis-priyanka-gandhi-moots-congress-going-solo-in-uttar-pradesh-in-2022/article29833959.ece.

Zoya Hasan, 'The Congress' moment of truth,' *The Hindu*, 11 August 2014, https://www.thehindu.com/opinion/lead/the-congress-moment-of-truth/article6301572.ece.

Aarthi Ramachandran, 'Congress: Portrait of a party in decline,' *Deccan Herald*, 11 July 2019, https://www.deccanherald.com/opinion/congress-portrait-of-a-party-in-decline-746460.html.

Nikhil Chakravartty, 'Indira Gandhi installed as president of break-away faction of Congress Party,' *India Today*, 31 January 1978, https://www.indiatoday.in/magazine/cover-story/story/19780131-indira-gandhi-installed-as-president-of-break-away-faction-of-congress-party-818678-2015-04-21.

Arun Kumar, 'How long would Uttar Pradesh CM Narayan Dutt Tewari survive the endemic in-fighting?' *India Today*, 31 January 1976, https://www.indiatoday.in/magazine/indiascope/story/19760131-how-long-would-uttar-pradesh-cm-narayan-dutt-tewari-survive-the-endemic-in-fighting-819568-2015-03-31.

5: The Caste-based Criminal Gangs of UP

Jyoti Yadav, 'Brahmin pride and pain flood Facebook after Vikas Dubey's encounter killing,' *The Print*, 10 July 2020, https://theprint.in/opinion/pov/brahmin-pride-pain-flood-facebook-vikas-dubey-encounter-killing/458417/.

Omar Rashid, 'Gangster Vikas Dubey shot dead in "exchange of fire",' *The Hindu*, 10 July 2020, https://www.thehindu.com/news/national/other-states/gangster-vikas-dubey-dead-says-up-police/article32038219.ece.

'Endgame, all in a week: This is gangster Vikas Dubey's story,' *The Tribune*, 11 July 2020, https://www.tribuneindia.com/news/nation/endgame-all-in-a-week-this-is-gangster-vikas-dubeys-story-110995.

Shobhaa De, 'Vikas Dubey Finale Worse Than C-Grade Thriller From 70s,' *NDTV*, 10 July 2020, https://www.ndtv.com/opinion/

vikas-dubey-story-merits-bad-film-with-akshay-kumar-by-shobhaa-de-2260393.

'Hansal Mehta confirms directing web series on gangster Vikas Dubey's life: "Development begins soon",' *Hindustan Times*, 10 August 2020, https://www.hindustantimes.com/tv/hansal-mehta-confirms-directing-web-series-on-gangster-vikas-dubey-s-life-development-begins-soon/story-JcNrrHpMKyU9k6V0xbeUYK.html.

Radhika Ramaseshan, 'What Vikas Dubey takes to the grave,' *Mumbai Mirror*, 12 July 2020, https://mumbaimirror.indiatimes.com/mumbai/cover-story/what-vikas-dubey-takes-to-the-grave/articleshow/76916610.cms?utm_source=contentofinterest&utm_medium=text&utm_campaign=cppst.

Rashme Sehgal, 'Gangsters, old and new, continue flourishing in Yogi Adityanath's Uttar Pradesh,' *National Herald*, 10 July 2020, https://www.nationalheraldindia.com/opinion/gangsters-old-and-new-continue-flourishing-in-yogi-adityanaths-uttar-pradesh.

'In Uttar Pradesh politics is proving to be a deadly game,' *India Today*, 3 March 2014, https://www.indiatoday.in/magazine/indiascope/story/19790930-in-uttar-pradesh-politics-is-proving-to-be-a-deadly-game-822527-2014-03-03.

Geetanjali Krishna, 'Holding Lucknow To Ransom,' *Business Standard*, 27 January 2013, https://www.business-standard.com/article/specials/holding-lucknow-to-ransom-198053001054_1.html.

Subhash Mishra, 'Increase in crime, mafia activity puts Uttar Pradesh CM Kalyan Singh on the defensive,' *India Today*, 6 July 1998, https://www.indiatoday.in/magazine/states/story/19980706-increase-in-crime-mafia-activity-puts-uttar-pradesh-cm-kalyan-singh-on-the-defensive-826566-1998-07-06.

Himanshu Tiwari, *Navbharat Times*, 14 December 2019, https://navbharattimes.indiatimes.com/metro/lucknow/crime/up-most-wanted-shooter-shri-prakash-shukla-crime-history-and-unique-story-about-his-single-picture/articleshow/72591362.cms.

Sanjay Bhatnagar, 'Guns, girls and gangs: After the Vikas Dubey encounter, a look at how the dons of UP operate,' *The Indian Express*, 19 July 2020, https://www.newindianexpress.com/magazine/2020/jul/19/guns-girls-and-gangs-after-the-vikas-dubey-encounter-a-look-at-how-the-dons-of-up-operate-2170729.html.

Rashmi Rajput, 'The murder that helped nab Abu Salem,' *The Indian Express*, 9 September 2017, https://indianexpress.com/article/opinion/1993-mumbai-serial-blasts-it-took-a-murder-a-globe-and-finally-a-map-to-nab-abu-salem-4834740/.

'1993 Mumbai serial blasts verdict today: How did Abu Salem meet Sanjay Dutt?' *Hindustan* Times, 17 June 2017, https://www.hindustantimes.com/mumbai-news/how-abu-salem-met-sanjay-dutt-became-1993-mumbai-serial-blasts-case-accused/story-IpyR19frESP2HVo3cD1MfN.html.

Manas Tiwari, 'Who is Abu Salem, what is his link with Dawood Ibrahim and role in 1993 Mumbai blast?' *Financial Express*, 7 September 2017, https://www.financialexpress.com/india-news/who-is-abu-salem-what-is-his-link-with-dawood-ibrahim-and-role-in-1993-mumbai-blast/845206/.

Jhinuk Sen, 'Gangs of UP: The bloody rivalry between Mukhtar Ansari and Brijesh Singh,' *Catch News*, 14 February 2017, http://www.catchnews.com/uttar-pradesh-election/gangs-of-up-the-bloody-rivalry-between-mukhtar-ansari-and-brijesh-singh-1485796708.html.

Rashme Sehgal, 'Gangsters, old and new, continue flourishing in Yogi Adityanath's Uttar Pradesh,' *National Herald*, 10 July 2020, https://www.nationalheraldindia.com/opinion/gangsters-old-and-new-continue-flourishing-in-yogi-adityanaths-uttar-pradesh.

Rashmi Rajput, 'The murder that helped nab Abu Salem,' *The Indian Express*, 9 September 2017, https://indianexpress.com/article/opinion/1993-mumbai-serial-blasts-it-took-a-murder-a-globe-and-finally-a-map-to-nab-abu-salem-4834740/.

Shekhar Iyer, 'It's parivar time for BJP in Azamgarh,' *Hindustan Times*, 13 January 2012, https://www.hindustantimes.com/india/it-s-parivar-time-for-bjp-in-azamgarh/story-Yf3spBO6gysOwWfqevbAHO.html.

Rajesh Joshi, 'Azamgarh's Guns for Hire,' *Outlook*, 8 September 1997, https://magazine.outlookindia.com/story/azamgarhs-guns-for-hire/204211.

'Brawn power,' *The Times of India*, 24 September 2011, https://timesofindia.indiatimes.com/city/lucknow/brawn-power/articleshow/10098572.cms.

'1993 Mumbai serial blasts verdict today: How did Abu Salem meet Sanjay Dutt?' *Hindustan Times*, 17 June 2017, https://www.hindustantimes.com/mumbai-news/how-abu-salem-met-sanjay-dutt-became-1993-mumbai-serial-blasts-case-accused/story-IpyR19frESP2HVo3cD1MfN.html.

https://en.calameo.com/read/000616136e22cc49c67e2.

Dilip Awasthi, 'Elusive bandit Dadua continues to outwit Uttar Pradesh police,' *India Today*, 31 July 1986, https://www.indiatoday.in/magazine/crime/story/19860731-elusive-bandit-dadua-continues-to-outwit-uttar-pradesh-police-801103-1986-07-31.

'Find dacoit's wife, win Rs 21 lakh!' *Rediff.com*, 31 July 2004, https://www.rediff.com/news/2004/jul/31up.htm.

6: The Polarization Plank

Rehan Fazal, *BBC News*, 10 October 2016, https://www.bbc.com/hindi/india-37602452.

Dinesh Shakya, *Patrika*, 14 March 2020, https://www.patrika.com/etawah-news/untold-story-of-bsp-founder-kanshi-ram-5890882/.

Saurabh Dwivedi, *The Lallantop,* 15 March 2019, https://www.thelallantop.com/tehkhana/dalit-icon-kaanshirams-life-politics-bsp-movemnet-and-the-legacy-given-to-mayawati/.

Ramachandra Guha, *Bharat: Nehru Ke Baad Duniya Ke Vishaaltam Loktantra Ka Itihaas* (New Delhi: Penguin India, 2012).

Javed M Ansari, 'As Mayawati becomes first Dalit chief minister of Uttar Pradesh, hopes rise in Badalpur,' *India Today*, 30 June 1995, https://www.indiatoday.in/magazine/cover-story/story/19950630-as-mayawati-becomes-first-dalit-chief-minister-of-uttar-pradesh-hopes-rise-in-badalpur-808385-1995-06-30.

Farzand Ahmed, 'Order to reopen Ram Janmabhoomi temple complex in Ayodhya sees tensions come to the boil,' *India Today*, 28 February 1986, https://www.indiatoday.in/magazine/religion/story/19860228-order-to-reopen-ram-janmabhoomi-temple-complex-in-ayodhya-sees-tensions-come-to-the-boil-800646-1986-02-28.

7: The Bastions

Aman Dwivedi, 'In Modi's "bastion" Varanasi, why is BJP running a whirlwind campaign?' *Financial Express*, 6 March 2017, https://

www.financialexpress.com/elections/uttar-pradesh-assembly-elections-2017/in-modis-bastion-varanasi-why-is-bjp-running-a-whirlwind-campaign/575476/.

Nilanjan Mukhopadhyay, 'Why Narendra Modi decided to contest from Varanasi,' *The Economic Times*, 17 March 2014, https://economictimes.indiatimes.com/news/politics-and-nation/why-narendra-modi-decided-to-contest-from-varanasi/articleshow/32165892.cms.

'Modi files nomination in Varanasi, invokes "Maa Durga",' *Hindustan Times*, 24 April 2014, https://www.hindustantimes.com/india/modi-files-nomination-in-varanasi-invokes-maa-ganga/story-UVRnxWGsliAI8SoJU4NIyM.html.

'The importance of Uttar Pradesh,' *The Hindu*, 19 March 2014, https://www.thehindu.com/opinion/editorial/the-importance-of-uttar-pradesh/article5801641.ece.

'VVIP constituency: 8 things PM Modi did for Varanasi,' *The Economic Times*, 26 April 2019, https://economictimes.indiatimes.com/news/elections/lok-sabha/india/vvip-constituency-8-things-pm-modi-did-for-varanasi/articleshow/69052002.cms.

Revati Laul, 'In Modi's Varanasi, dissent is brewing as development promises fail and divisions grow,' *Scroll.in,* 20 May 2019, https://scroll.in/article/924007/in-modis-varanasi-a-quiet-dissent-is-brewing-as-development-promises-fail-and-divisions-grow.

Sudhir Kumar, 'Development Varanasi, Advantage Modi?' *Hindustan Times,* 11 December 2018, https://www.hindustantimes.com/lucknow/development-varanasi-advantage-modi/story-PnQYmjYit3Qyobvy6lXtbO.html.

Shuchi Bansal, 'Some questions, but no contest in Narendra Modi's Varanasi,' *Mint*, 17 May 2019, https://www.livemint.com/elections/

lok-sabha-elections/some-questions-but-no-contest-in-narendra-modi-s-varanasi-1558033740946.html.

'Clean Ganga project fails to make progress,' *The Hindu*, 9 January 2018, https://www.thehindubusinessline.com/economy/clean-ganga-project-fails-to-make-progress/article9996997.ece.

'People regret voting against Indira Gandhi in Rae Bareli,' *India Today*, 15 September 1977, https://www.indiatoday.in/magazine/cover-story/story/19770915-people-regret-voting-against-indira-gandhi-in-rae-bareli-823883-2014-09-02.

Prashant K. Nanda, 'Ground Zero: The past, present and the future,' *Mint*, 22 June 2015, https://www.livemint.com/Politics/zQU05QzodYPSfwhuhruLOL/Ground-Zero-The-past-present-and-the-future.html.

Bertil Falk, 'How Rae Bareli came to love and respect Feroze Gandhi and his family,' *The Print*, 12 September 2018, https://theprint.in/pageturner/how-rae-bareli-came-to-love-and-respect-feroze-gandhi-and-his-family/116589/.

'Industries shut down in Gandhi land,' *DNA*, 19 November 2013, https://www.dnaindia.com/india/report-industries-shut-down-in-gandhi-land-1149353.

Mohd Faisal Fareed, 'Saifai: Rs 300-cr to beautify Mulayam's native village of 7,000 people,' *The Indian Express*, 28 March 2016, https://indianexpress.com/article/cities/lucknow/saifai-rs-300-cr-to-beautify-mulayams-native-village-of-7000-people/.

Piyush Babele, 'Akhilesh repays his debt to Saifai voters,' *India Today*, 16 June 2012, https://www.indiatoday.in/magazine/nation/story/20120625-akhilesh-yadav-samajwadi-party-saifai-development-works-758780-2012-06-16.

Geeta Pandey, 'Akhilesh Yadav: the new chief minister of Uttar Pradesh,' *BBC News*, 15 March 2012, https://www.bbc.com/news/world-asia-india-17336261.

'Saifai to get international cricket stadium,' *The Indian Express*, 5 August 2015, https://indianexpress.com/article/cities/lucknow/saifai-to-get-international-cricket-stadium/.

Namita Bajpai, 'Lucknow ushers into Metro era; Yogi Adityanath, Akhilesh Yadav engage in Twitter war for credit,' *The Indian Express*, 5 September 2017, https://www.newindianexpress.com/nation/2017/sep/05/lucknow-ushers-into-metro-era-yogi-adityanath-akhilesh-yadav-engage-in-twitter-war-for-credit-1652866.html.

'Foundation stone laid for Lucknow Metro project,' *The Hindu*, 3 March 2014, https://www.thehindubusinessline.com/news/national/foundation-stone-laid-for-lucknow-metro-project/article23170994.ece.

Purnima S. Tripathi, 'Enigmatic forever,' *The Hindu*, https://frontline.thehindu.com/other/obituary/article24800325.ece.

Ravi S. Dutta, 'Saifai revisited: Sitting on the edge, ear to the ground,' *Hindustan Times*, 18 February 2017, https://www.hindustantimes.com/lucknow/saifai-revisited-sitting-on-the-edge-ear-to-the-ground/story-8alzYgRxiRFH90AvUNQQpJ.html.

Piyush Srivastava, 'Maya's bounty for parks but peanuts for poor Bundelkhand,' *India Today*, 12 August 2010, https://www.indiatoday.in/india/north/story/mayas-bounty-for-parks-but-peanuts-for-poor-bundelkhand-80225-2010-08-12.

Smita Gupta, 'Mayawati's cleverly crafted pre-election strategy,' *The Hindu*, 16 November 2011, https://www.thehindu.com/news/national/mayawatis-cleverly-crafted-preelection-strategy/article2630995.ece.

Man Mohan Rai, 'Mayawati writes to PM... opposes formation of Bundelkhand Authority,' *The Economic Times*, 31 July 2009, https://economictimes.indiatimes.com/news/politics-and-nation/mayawati-writes-to-pm-opposes-formation-of-bundelkhand-authority/articleshow/4843363.cms.

'Challenged by Rahul Gandhi, Mayawati to tour Bundelkhand,' *DNA*, 19 November 2013, https://www.dnaindia.com/india/report-challenged-by-rahul-gandhi-mayawati-to-tour-bundelkhand-1146233.

Ratan Mani Lal, 'In backward Bundelkhand, the BSP has a lot at stake,' *Firstpost*, 29 April 2014, https://www.firstpost.com/politics/in-backward-bundelkhand-the-bsp-has-a-lot-at-stake-1502223.html.

Aarti Dhar, 'Non-Dalit voters hold the key in Bundelkhand,' *The Hindu*, 23 February 2012, https://www.thehindu.com/news/national/other-states/nondalit-voters-hold-the-key-in-bundelkhand/article2920103.ece.

Aditi Vatsa, 'The elephant in the room: Why Mayawati's statues are under Supreme Court lens,' *The Print*, 9 February 2019, https://theprint.in/theprint-essential/the-elephant-in-the-room-why-mayawatis-statues-are-under-supreme-court-lens/190179/.

NDTV India, 10 December 2015, https://ndtv.in/india-news/grass-weeds-traditional-diet-how-up-government-covered-up-ndtv-report-on-hunger-1253143.

'Government releases Rs 40,000 crore under Bundelkhand package,' *The Economic Times*, 7 August 2015, https://economictimes.indiatimes.com/news/economy/policy/government-releases-rs-40000-crore-under-bundelkhand-package/articleshow/48390468.cms?from=mdr.

8: BJP Is Ram Bharose

'1990-L.K. Advani's rath yatra: Chariot of fire,' *India Today,* 28 December 2009, https://www.indiatoday.in/magazine/cover-story/story/20091228-1990-l.k.-advanis-rath-yatra-chariot-of-fire-741621-2009-12-24.

Kabir Agarwal, 'L.K. Advani, the Provocateur in Chief,' *The Wire*, 9 November 2019, https://thewire.in/politics/the-provocateur-in-chief-l-k-advani.

Sharat Pradhan, 'At Ayodhya Bhoomi Pujan, Modi Became All-in-One; Proper Rituals Not Followed, Allege Pundits,' *The Wire*, 7 August 2020, https://thewire.in/politics/ayodhya-bhoomi-pujan-narendra-modi-priests-pundits.

Sai Manish, 'Babri demolition, 25 years on: BJP's transition from Ram to reform to Ram,' *Business Standard,* 6 August 2019, https://www.business-standard.com/article/politics/babri-demolition-25-years-on-bjp-s-transition-from-ram-to-reform-to-ram-117120100186_1.html.

Dilip Awasthi, 'Kalyan Singh treads cautiously, avoiding trouble,' *India Today,* 31 July 1991, https://www.indiatoday.in/magazine/indiascope/story/19910731-kalyan-singh-treads-cautiously-avoiding-trouble-814629-1991-07-31.

Prabhash K. Dutta, 'Ayodhya: When Mulayam Singh Yadav ordered police firing on karsevaks heading to Babri Masjid,' *India Today*, 30 October 2019, https://www.indiatoday.in/india/story/ayodhya-when-mulayam-singh-yadav-ordered-police-firing-on-karsevaks-heading-to-babri-masjid-1614033-2019-10-30.

'1990: L.K. Advani's rath yatra: Chariot of fire,' *India Today,* 28 December 2009, https://www.indiatoday.in/magazine/cover-story/story/20091228-1990-l.k.-advanis-rath-yatra-chariot-of-fire-741621-2009-12-24.

9: The Switchers

https://www.bhaskar.com/news/UP-LUCK-up-political-history-phenomenon-tarnished-dignity-4791037-PHO.html.

Atul Chandra, '1991-2017: The Epic Saga Of Elections In Uttar Pradesh,' *Swarajya,* 4 February 2017, https://swarajyamag.com/politics/1991-2017-the-epic-saga-of-elections-in-uttar-pradesh.

https://www.patrika.com/lucknow-news/bjp-congress-and-sp-leaders-joined-bjp-for-success-in-up-election-2017-hindi-news-1528829/.

Ruhi Tiwari, *The Print,* 22 March 2019, https://hindi.theprint.in/2019-loksabha-election/25-percent-of-bjps-ministers-in-states-are-defectors/51386/.

Ashish Misra, 'Season of defection begins in UP, BSP worst hit,' *India Today,* 2 March 2021, https://www.indiatoday.in/india-today-insight/story/season-of-defection-begins-in-up-bsp-worst-hit-1774486-2021-03-02.

Satyagrah, 31 July 2019, https://satyagrah.scroll.in/article/130369/dal-badal-bhartiya-loktantra-rajniti-congress-bjp-indira-gandhi.

Bhavdeep Kang, 'Together Again!' *Outlook,* 2 April 1997, https://magazine.outlookindia.com/story/together-again/203288.

'UP to get single party govt after 14 years,' *Outlook,* 11 May 2007, https://www.outlookindia.com/newswire/story/up-to-get-single-party-govt-after-14-years/472323.

Sharat Pradhan, 'Mayawati eats words, Kalyan Singh swallows bitter pills to keep BJP-BSP alliance going,' *Rediff.com*, http://www.rediff.com/news/may/09up.htm.

Sharat Pradhan, 'BSP withdraws support to UP govt,' *Rediff.com*, https://www.rediff.com/news/oct/19up.htm.

Swapan Dasgupta, Subhash Mishra and Farzand Ahmed, 'Political norms take a beating as splits, violence and subterfuge take over,' *India Today*, 3 November 1997, https://www.indiatoday.in/magazine/cover-story/story/19971103-political-norms-take-a-beating-as-splits-violence-and-subterfuge-take-over-830846-1997-11-03.

Subhash Mishra, 'Mayawati to ensure Kalyan Singh pursues her policies if he becomes UP chief minister,' *India Today*, 8 September 1997, https://www.indiatoday.in/magazine/states/story/19970901-mayawati-to-ensure-kalyan-singh-pursues-her-policies-if-he-becomes-up-chief-minister-830469-1997-09-08.

10: The Agrarian Crisis

G.R. Saini, 'Green Revolution and the Distribution of Farm Incomes,' *Economic and Political Weekly*, Vol. 11, No. 13 (1976): 17–22, http://www.jstor.org/stable/4364489.

Smriti Verma, Ashok Gulati and Siraj Hussain, 'Doubling Agricultural Growth in Uttar Pradesh: Sources and Drivers of Agricultural Growth and Policy Lessons,' *Indian Council for Research on International Economic Relations*, No. 335 (March 2017), https://icrier.org/pdf/Working_Paper_335.pdf.

Khursheed A. Khan, 'Crisis of Agriculture in Uttar Pradesh: From Apprehension to Actuality,' *Journal of Economics and Sustainable Development*, Vol. 5, No. 11 (2014): 150–60, https://core.ac.uk/download/pdf/234646429.pdf.

Rakesh Raman and Khursheed Ahmad Khan, 'Crisis of Agriculture in Uttar Pradesh: Investigating Acuteness & Antecedents,' *Amity*

Journal of Agribusiness, Vol. 2, No. 1 (2017): 13–27, https://amity.edu/UserFiles/admaa/c5228Paper%202.pdf.

Gaurav Kadam, 'Farmers' Protest: In 1988, BKU leader Rakesh Tikait's father Mahendra Singh brought Rajiv Gandhi govt to its knees,' *The Free Press Journal,* 31 January 2021, https://www.freepressjournal.in/india/farmers-protest-in-1988-bku-leader-rakesh-tikaits-father-mahendra-singh-brought-rajiv-gandhi-govt-to-its-knees.

Indranil De and Sanjib Pohit, 'Rich farmers dominate farm protests in India. It's happening since Charan Singh days,' *The Print,* 30 September 2020, https://theprint.in/opinion/rich-farmers-dominate-farm-protests-in-india-its-happening-since-charan-singh-days/513027/.

'MSP, Debt Crisis: Why Farmers in Western UP Are Protesting Against Farm Laws,' *News Click,* 30 November 2020, https://www.newsclick.in/MSP-debt-crisis-farmers-western-UP-protesting-farm-laws.

Divya Trivedi, 'Farmers in Uttar Pradesh protest against farm laws amid grave agrarian crisis,' *Frontline,* 6 November 2020, https://frontline.thehindu.com/cover-story/farmer-in-deep-crisis/article32882362.ece.

Sudipto Mundle, 'Agrarian crisis: the challenge of a small farmer economy,' *Mint,* 21 July 2017, https://www.livemint.com/Opinion/Y3Fp6CcumJhRIEwl2WeUMM/Agrarian-crisis-the-challenge-of-a-small-farmer-economy.html.

Moushumi Das Gupta, 'Huge concern that Covid hit UP rural areas where medical infra is inadequate, minister says,' *The Print,* 29 April 2021, https://theprint.in/india/huge-concern-that-covid-hit-up-rural-areas-where-medical-infra-is-inadequate-minister-says/648067/.

Saurabh Chauhan, 'UP population far from exploding, but still soaring,' *Hindustan Times,* 23 September 2019, https://www.hindustantimes.com/lucknow/up-population-far-from-exploding-but-still-soaring/story-7LCpyIRiqewRGv5Pr8ta4K.html.

Jagadish Shettigar and Pooja Misra, 'Wake-up call for India's healthcare infrastructure,' *Mint,* 25 May 2021, https://www.livemint.com/news/india/wakeup-call-for-india-s-healthcare-infrastructure-11621961832421.html.

Moushumi Das Gupta, 'In Yogi's UP, expressways are scripting silent transformation in state known for poor road infra,' *The Print,* 13 April 2021, https://theprint.in/india/governance/in-yogis-up-expressways-are-scripting-silent-transformation-in-state-known-for-poor-road-infra/638384/.

Neha Lalchandani, 'PM Narendra Modi lauds Uttar Pradesh's industrial development & ease of doing business,' *The Times of India,* 3 July 2021, https://timesofindia.indiatimes.com/city/lucknow/pm-modi-lauds-ups-industrial-devpt-ease-of-doing-business/articleshow/84081013.cms.

Subhash Mishra, 'Unemployment rate dips to 4.1% in Uttar Pradesh: CMIE,' *The Times of India,* 4 March 2021, https://timesofindia.indiatimes.com/city/lucknow/unemployment-rate-dips-to-4-1-in-up-cmie/articleshow/81320713.cms.

Uttar Pradesh is scripting a new saga of economic transformation,' *The Times of India,* 16 March 2021, https://timesofindia.indiatimes.com/city/lucknow/uttar-pradesh-is-scripting-a-new-saga-of-economic-transformation/articleshow/81520509.cms.

Appendix

Automatic Zoom

Caste Sentiment Rears Head In U. P.: PROBLEM FOR <span ...
Our Own Correspondent
The Times of India (1861-current); Aug 15, 1951; ProQuest Historical Newspapers: The Times of India
pg. 3

Caste Sentiment Rears Head In U. P.

PROBLEM FOR CONGRESS IN RURAL AREAS

From Our Own Correspondent

LUCKNOW.

TO proceed on the presumption that the Congress will again be returned to power in Uttar Pradesh will not be unwarranted. Whatever be the demands of the election propaganda and the need to build up party morale—Mr. Rafi Ahmed Kidwai recently said at a meeting of workers of the Kisan Mazdoor Praja Party that it would sweep the polls, no one in private seriously contests that the Con-

tion, that they will win 80 per cent. of the 430 seats in the Lower House of the State Legis-

Automatic Zoom

POONA PACT: GANDHI TO CONSULT LEADERS OF DEPRESSED CLASSES
The Times of India (1861-current); May 10, 1933; ProQuest Historical Newspapers: The Times of India
pg. 9

POONA PACT

GANDHI TO CONSULT LEADERS OF DEPRESSED CLASSES

AHMEDABAD, May 9.

"If the question of changing the Poona Pact arises again, I shall certainly consult other Harijan leaders" writes Mr. Gandhi in the course of a letter to Mr. Rajbhoj of Poona, a depressed classes leader, who wrote to Mr. Gandhi advising him to call a meeting of Harijan leaders to consider the change in the Poona Pact as proposed by Dr. Ambedkar.

Automatic Zoom

Pandit Pant's Expected Inclusion In Centre: DISTURBING EFFECT ON POLITICAL SCENE Utt
The Times of India News Service
The Times of India (1861-current); Nov 26, 1954; ProQuest Historical Newspapers: The Times of India
pg. 9

Pandit Pant's Expected Inclusion In Centre

DISTURBING EFFECT ON POLITICAL SCENE

"The Times of India" News Service

LUCKNOW, November 24.

THE expecfed inclusion of U. P.'s Chief Minister, Pandit Govind Ballabh Pant, in the Central Cabinet is having a disturbing effect on the State's comparatively tranquil political scene.

Controversy over the merits of the change has been

Automatic Zoom

MR. NEHRU'S "NO": M.L.A.S WANT PANDIT <SPAN CLASS="HIT">PANT</SPAN> IN U
The Times of India News Service
The Times of India (1861-current); Nov 26, 1954; ProQuest Historical Newspapers: The Times of India
pg. 8

MR. NEHRU'S "NO" M.L.A.s Want Pandit Pant In U. P.

"The Times of India" News Service

LUCKNOW, November 24: The inclusion of Pandit Govind Ballabh Pant, U.P.'s Chief Minister, in the Central Cabinet is now certain, according to authoritative sources here.

The Prime Minister, Mr. Nehru, it is learnt, brushed aside yesterday a request of a group of six U.P. legislators to let Pandit Pant continue as Chief Minister of the State.

The group, which included five

Automatic Zoom

CHARAN SINGH WANTS TO BE RELIEVED OF S.V.D. LEADERSHIP
The Times of India News Service
The Times of India (1861-current); Aug 17, 1967; ProQuest Historical Newspapers: The Times of India
pg. 1

CHARAN SINGH WANTS TO BE RELIEVED OF S.V.D. LEADERSHIP

"The Times of India" News Service

LUCKNOW, August 16.

THE Chief Minister, Mr. Charan Singh, is reliably learnt to have written to Mr. Ugra Sen, secretary of the co-ordination committee of the ruling Samyukta Vidhayak Dal, informing him that he would like to be relieved of the burden of leading the party and suggesting that the SVD should elect a new leader.

Mr. Charan Singh will, however, continue to be a member of the

kash, Deputy Chief Minister (Jan Sangh), in which he had questioned the right of the Cabinet and of the Chief Minister to approve nominations to committees.

Automatic Zoom

CHARAN RESIGNS: ASSEMBLY SESSION IS OFF
The Times of India News Service
The Times of India (1861-current); Feb 18, 1968; ProQuest Historical Newspapers: The Times of India
pg. 1

CHARAN RESIGNS: ASSEMBLY SESSION IS OFF

"The Times of India" News Service

LUCKNOW, February 17.

THE Governor, Mr. B. Gopala Reddy, today accepted the resignation of the Chief Minister, Mr. Charan Singh, and asked him to continue as the care-taker Chief Minister until he could make fresh arrangements to run the Government.

Automatic Zoom

Kalyan downplays Ayodhya

By DEEPAK GIDWANI
The Times of India News Service

RAM SANEHI GHAT
(Bara Banki), Sept. 21.

NEXT to the banks of the river Kalyani in this district, the chief minister, Mr Kalyan Singh, yesterday spelt out a six-point plan of action (PoA) which, he said, his government would implement rigorously. Ironically, the construction of the Ram temple in Ayodhya got the last ranking in the chief minister's latest PoA.

The chief minister was rounding off his hectic helicopter trip here this evening. Earlier, he had addressed public meetings at Lalganj (Rae Bareli) and in Unnao. At all the meetings, the chief minister repeated his six-point strategy — in the same sequence.

As the chief minister's helicopter became visible on the distant horizon in Bara Banki, the crowds

minister was seemingly fighting shy of the issue. He thundered: "No force on earth can stop the temple construction", but did not extend any commitment.

His speech at the meetings was invariably laced with the usual rhetoric on the issue which swept the BJP to power in the state. He said that if the Centre dismissed the BJP government, it would imperial the safety and security of the disputed structure and of the Central government too. The chief minister's speech was unusually offensive, specially when he referred to the Centre's role in the Ayodhya issue.

He warned the Prime Minister to consider the consequences before taking any decisive step in this regard. Referring to the Janata Dal president, Mr S. R. Bommai's visit to Ayodhya earlier this year, he said that the temple construction had been stalled because of "such

Automatic Zoom

Mulayam terrorising BSP MLAs to side with SP, alleges Mayawati
P B VarmaThe Times of India News Service
The Times of India (1861-current); Jun 4, 1995; ProQuest Historical Newspapers: The Times of India
pg. 24

Mulayam terrorising BSP MLAs to side with SP, alleges Mayawati

By P. B. Varma
The Times of India News Service

LUCKNOW, June 3.

Bahujan Samaj Party (BSP) general secretary Mayawati, known for her boldness, is finding the way to chief ministership quite thorny.

In an interview, she alleged that her party legislators were being terrorised to express their support to the Samajwadi Party (SP) government, which had been reduced to a minority after the withdrawal of BSP support. She claimed that SP MLAs, had expressed their willingness to join hands with the BSP. Following are excerpts from the interview:

What are the main factors which forced your party to withdraw support and thus break the SP-BSP coalition government in the state?

We had to withdraw support due to continuing atrocities on the scheduled castes, the scheduled tribes and the weaker sections in Uttar Pradesh. There was a total breakdown of law and order and the government had failed miserably in providing relief to the weaker sections in pursuance of our policy of social justice in the distribution of land. Besides, the SP had resorted to malpractices and rigging in the panchayat elections and also in the subsequent by-elections held for the state assembly.

Which political parties have expressed their firm support, if you are invited to form the government?

The BJP and the Janata Dal have informed the governor about their support. N.D. Tiwari has promised his full support and has told me that necessary formalities in this connection would be completed today at the meeting of the Congress Working Committee (CWC), which is being held at Delhi. Besides, I had a talk with UPCC president Jitendra Prasad on the telephone. He has also condemned last evening's incident in which our MLAs were beaten up and kidnapped from the state guest house and has assured me that the question of giving support to our party would be discussed at the CWC meeting.

What happened at the state guest house last evening? Was anyone beaten up? Do you still feel any danger from those persons?

I was holding a meeting of my party legislators at the state guest house which was attended by all, except two or three MLAs. As soon as I finished the meeting and retired to my room in the guest house along with some MLAs, several SP legislators, accompanied by a large number of anti-social elements, entered the guest house raising slogans, and started beating up the BSP MLAs. They forcibly took away five of our legislators while others ran helter-skelter to save themselves. The police throughout stood as a mute spectator. One of our MLAs, Mewa Lal Bagi, was also being forced to get into a car by the kidnappers. But at the intervention of the security-men of another MLA of our party, who had prevented the driver from starting the car, Mr Bagi got an opportunity to escape from there. The electricity of the guest house was switched off for about three hours, from 6 to 9 p.m., due to which the place was plunged into darkness.

Who are the legislators who were kidnapped in this incident?

The MLAs kidnapped from this place last evening are Ram Achal Rajbhar, Sarnai Ram, Akshaibar Bharti, Jaganmath Chaudhary and Rajendra Kumar. Besides several other BSP MLAs have been kidnapped either from their residences or while they were moving out. The whereabouts of some of them are not known.

Some MLAs belonging to your party, led by Raj Bahadur, have expressed their allegiance to Mulayam Singh Yadav. What have you to say about them?

They have been made to do so at gun point. Their lives are in danger. I have requested the governor to ensure their safe return to us. Former BSP minister Deena Nath Bhaskar was given an allurement of Rs 50 lakh and a car by Mr Yadav. However, when he declined this offer, they threatened him with dire consequences. Mr Bhaskar is now hiding somewhere to save his life.

Have you been able to get the support of some SP MLAs?

Disgusted with the last evening's hooliganism committed by the SP legislators and other anti-social elements, SP MLA Praveen Kumar Aron has pledged his support to me along with six other MLAs of his party. He talked to me on phone last night and told me that he would be holding a press conference at Delhi today. Besides these MLAs, about 20 other SP legislators have also promised to extend their support to us on the floor of the house. They are holding their separate meetings today. I do not want to disclose their names just now otherwise their lives would be in danger.

Would your party contest the next elections in alliance with the BJP?

This is a question which we will think over when the time comes.

Automatic Zoom

RajiV launches poll drive
the Times of India News Service
The Times of India (1861-current); Nov 4, 1989; ProQuest Historical Newspapers: The Times of India
pg. 17

Rajiv launches poll drive

The Times of India News Service

FAIZABAD, November 3: The Prime Minister, Mr Rajiv Gandhi, today launched his party's election campaign from here and called upon the people to vote for the Congress if they wanted "Ram Rajya."

Addressing a well-attended public meeting in a sprawling field, barely six km from Lord Rama's birthplace at Ayodhya, Mr Gandhi said it was only the Congress which could bring back "Ram rajya" in the country.

Making a subtle reference to communal trouble erupting repeatedly on account of the disputed shrine in the neighbourhood, the Prime Minister made a vehement attack on forces that were attempting at spreading communalism.

He said communalism would only weaken the nation and hence deserved to be curbed with a heavy hand.

Mr Gandhi blamed the opposition for encouraging communal and dis-

Index

Acknowledgements

There was never any doubt in my mind that putting together a book on Uttar Pradesh, in large parts based on my own reporting, would be an intense and complex task. And from Day 1 I knew that I would need to involve the notable few who have known, studied, analysed and reported on the state for years, including those who offer a perspective different from my own. So, my heartfelt thanks to those who took out their valuable time to engage with me.

Noted senior journalist Hemant Sharma's book on Ayodhya, an eyewitness account of the Babri Masjid demolition, is a unique and readable narrative. He and I had many discussions on the rise of the BJP from the early days of the Ram Janmabhoomi movement. On the days of Congress dominance and its decline, I spoke to my old friend, author and astute political journalist Rasheed Kidwai. Nirmal Pathak, another old friend and fine journalist, has tracked the impact of Lucknow on Delhi for decades. Sharad Pradhan has seen UP through the decades and offered helpful inputs. With senior journalist Brajesh Shukla, who was formerly with *Dainik Jagran*, I discussed caste angles and many other developments in the state.

My thanks to my friend Avinash Pandey, CEO, ABP Network, who, despite his tight schedules, gave some critical feedback and a different perspective on a few chapters. Also, ABP's Mihir Ranjan, who has spent many years working in Lucknow, offered important comments on the chapter on the caste-based criminal gangs of UP.

Naturally, the book encompasses over two decades of my own reporting on UP, mainly done for NDTV. So, my heartfelt thanks to Radhika and Prannoy Roy.

A special mention for my researcher, Abhinava Srivastav, who kept working on the book through the difficult pandemic time and followed my schedules and deadlines. Being from UP himself, he grasped the central theme of the book very well and did a fine job of going back and forth to further research the new points I raised.

And, finally, the 'D Gang'—a group of immensely talented and wonderful people from Dehradun. My dear friend Manu Gaur tirelessly works on the significant issue of population, a topic I discussed several times with him in my shows. He guided me to a place where I could lock myself up and complete the Preface on why I wrote this book. Abhinav Kumar, a wonderful old friend, an exceptionally sharp mind and a senior cop in Uttarakhand, comes from Bareilly in UP. His insights and arguments with me helped frame parts of the book. The warm Ali Khan Saab, a poetry and music lover, made some of my evenings in Dehradun special and relaxing. My thanks to all of them. My discussions with them brought back stories from my time in UP which enriched the book.

About the Author

Abhigyan Prakash is an award-winning senior journalist and columnist and has been an iconic frontline face pioneering news television in India. In a career spanning over two decades, he has hosted many flagship shows for NDTV as one of its key editors and has reported on and analysed UP and national politics. Currently, he is Senior Consultant, ABP News, and its national affairs expert.